RAISING A DAUGHTER
in this 21st Century India

From Craddle to Marriage and After

RAISING A DAUGHTER
in this 21st Century India
From Craddle to Marriage and After

Rupa Chatterjee

V&S PUBLISHERS

Published by:

F-2/16, Ansari Road, Daryaganj, New Delhi-110002
☎ 011-23240026, 011-23240027 • *Fax:* 011-23240028
Email: info@vspublishers.com • *Website:* www.vspublishers.com

Branch : Hyderabad
5-1-707/1, Brij Bhawan (Beside Central Bank of India Lane)
Bank Street, Koti, Hyderabad - 500 095.
☎ 040-24737290.
E-mail: vspublishershyd@gmail.com

Follow us on:

For any assistance sms **VSPUB** to **56161**
All books available at **www.vspublishers.com**

© Copyright: V&S Publishers
ISBN 978-93-813846-6-4
Edition 2013

The Copyright of this book, as well as all matter contained herein (including illustrations) rests with the Publishers. No person shall copy the name of the book, its title design, matter and illustrations in any form and in any language, totally or partially or in any distorted form. Anybody doing so shall face legal action and will be responsible for damages.

Printed at : Param Offseters, Okhla, New Delhi-110020

ଔ✳✳ଓ

Dedicated to

"My Mother, Gauri Banerji
My Daughters, Romira & Ronita
And
Grand daughter, Riya"

ଔ✳✳ଓ

Preface for the Revised Edition

Although some of what I wrote in the previous edition still holds true, the winds of change sweeping into our society have strengthened in the past six years and many new avenues and opportunities are opening up to our daughters, which were not there even six years ago. Along with economic liberalization, the spread of education and the growth of television, new doors of opportunity are available to our daughters. From one Kiran Bedi there are now hundreds of them in the police forces, army, navy and air force. A girl of Indian origin in the United States, Kalyani Chawla, was part of the space programme. Reality tv has crept into our drawing rooms and parents from small towns of India are allowing their young daughters to participate in song and dance competitions or beauty pageants, which would not have happened even five years ago. For many mothers, not only is the *ghoongat* out, but even they are getting into jeans and skirts and thumbing their nose at convention. The divorce rate is up, careers are paramount and motherhood is taking a back seat in the present scheme of things. Changes are taking place very swiftly, but it is necessary to step back and take a look at what we are doing and what awaits us in the future. While society is changing, human nature and biology remains, to some extent, constant. The instinct to find a partner and nurture comes up as nature designed it to do.

Thus, the question arises is how much should we change as parents and as daughters to survive in the present scenario? If life is all about balance and juggling multiple roles and responsibilities, then my revised edition will try to update the reader on the new situations arising out of our changing society and how we can raise and help our daughters in the present day.

Rupa Chatterjee
January 2010

Contents

	Introduction	09
1.	The Girl Child through the ages	13
2.	Prevalent Attitudes Towards the Girl-child	18
3.	The Girl-child at Home	25
4.	Handling Teenagers	43
5.	Educating Your Daughter	51
6.	A Daughter's Socio-cultural and Sartorial Education	57
7.	Some New Hazards of Bringing Up a Daughter	60
8.	A Daughter's Physical and Mental Well-being	74
9.	The Role of Physical Fitness	88
10.	Emotional Well-being	95
11.	Handling Puberty and its Problems	99
12.	The Queen of the Kitchen	105
13.	Career Options and Economic Compulsions	109
14.	Living with your working daughter	113
15.	Marriage and Motherhood	118
16.	Inheritance, Dowry and Divorce	144

Introduction

Until the last three decades of the 20th century, women throughout the world were placed in a special category – to be protected, cosseted, respected, revered, or discriminated against and exploited, as the situation warranted.

Till the mid-1960s, women all over the world were expected to fulfil their designated traditional roles in society which encompassed, as the Germans put it, "children, the kitchen and the church". Although history is full of instances of learned women and powerful queens from Vedic India to Victorian England, women by and large played a secondary role in society. A woman's ultimate aim was to have a 'good' marriage, as wealth, power and social prestige all emanated from the man and his status in society. The concept of a woman having her own identity and independent status simply did not exist.

After the First World War, when women were forced to help in the war effort and even take up jobs in factories, the Women's Suffragette Movement in the United States and England sought to obtain the right to vote. Despite their image of being 'advanced' and 'modern', women in Western societies were as dominated upon as their sisters elsewhere. During the Middle Ages, though chivalry was the order of the day, knights going on Crusades bound their wives with a chastity belt. Even as men fought duels to maintain the honour of their ladies, clerics asked, "Do women have souls?"

Even today, in many so-called modern and civilised cultures there are separate norms for men and women. For example, even in 21st century Japan, a girl cannot ascend the throne. The

Japanese ruler, believed to be a direct descendant of the Sun God, can only be male. In many Western countries, men and women do not receive equal pay for equal work and in Switzerland, women had not received the right to vote until the early 1990s.

For many centuries, the pattern of women's lives remained the same. Education for them was not considered important. Beauty, docility, domestic skills, obedience and patience were necessary virtues that had to be cultivated. Divorce was virtually unheard of and strong social strictures ensured that marriage was a permanent bond.

Although the Women's Liberation Movement of the 1960s, along with the emancipating effect of the birth control pill, forced a radical change in Western societies, in other parts of the world the effect has not been so dramatic. Yes, women are more educated and seek to utilise their education to become professionals and financially independent, but the home and family are still given importance, particularly in Indian society. Since India moves in several centuries at the same time, there are still many in the remote areas who bring up the girl-child as had been done over the millennium, with few concessions to modernity.

But in general, as the Taliban experience in Afghanistan has proved, the clock cannot be turned back to the medieval ages – some concessions have to be made to modernity and the winds of change are seeping in, no matter how slowly.

In order to bring up one's daughter in 21st century India, it is necessary to do what Indian society is known for, which is to achieve a fusion between the best of tradition and modernity, so that our daughters can achieve a pivotal role in the future of both the country and our family system. Individuals cannot function in a vacuum, so it is essential that the girl-child be brought up in a way that combines the best from the past in order to fulfill the challenges of the unknown future, without compromising on one's values and traditions.

This book seeks to offer balanced guidelines on the best ways of bringing up a daughter in present-day India. Thus, a broad gamut of topics have been touched upon. Sometimes the reader may find that the author is judgmental, at other times, liberal. This is because in today's fast-changing environment a rigid stance may be counterproductive, since girls are now being subjected to many influences that were not prevalent in an earlier era, such as excessive peer pressure, exposure to the media and the influence of the fashion industry.

Thus, it requires a great deal of maturity and tactful handling to exercise some influence over our children and to guide them in successfully tackling the multifarious roles that they face in the present world – as daughters, students, career women, wives, mothers and mothers-in-law. I do hope this book achieves that objective in some small measure.

Lastly, my special thanks to Mrs Tanushree Podder for her tips and suggestions and for contributing Chapter 11, Handling Puberty and its Problems.

Rupa Chatterjee

The Girl Child through the ages

𝒥n all traditional societies of the world, there were circumstances that favoured the birth of a male child, and India was no exception to this bias. While women in Vedic India had equal rights to education, the sanction to perform religious ceremonies and the freedom to select her husband at a *swayamvar*, there was a gradual deterioration in her position with the passage of time.

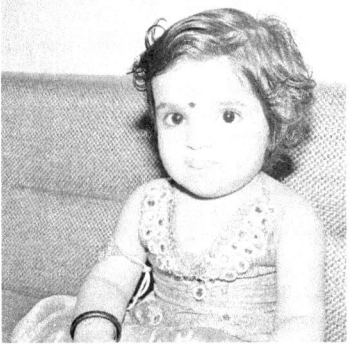

The situation reached its nadir between the 14th and 19th centuries, when child marriage, *sati* and *purdah* became the order of the day. Manu's dictat saw her position in society deteriorate further. The law giver Manu opined that from the cradle to the grave, a woman had to be under constant male supervision – at first that of her father, then her husband and finally, in old age, her son. Gradually, as her position in society declined, at home too, certain curbs were placed on her development.

The obsession to protect women stemmed from the frequency of foreign invasions and the abduction of women as part of the spoils of war during military campaigns. Many of the ostensibly restrictive measures stemmed from a desire to protect the girl-child from the horrors of rape and abduction indulged in by the invading armies from Persia, Afghanistan and Mongolia. The evil practice of *sati* had its origins in this historical reality, in which women preferred to ritualistically immolate themselves (*Jauhar*), rather than be carried off as part of the harem of invading rulers. The story of Rani Padmini of Chittor and the desire of Alauddin Khilji to win her over is a case in point.

Hitherto, Indian kings had waged war according to certain humane rules and norms, as all of them believed that the law of the *Dharmasastras* to be sacrosanct. Regardless of the provocation, the shrine, the Brahmin and the cow were never to be touched. Since warfare was a special privilege of the martial class, harassment of the civilian population was regarded as a serious breach of the code of conduct. Kshatriyas respected women, hence their abduction and dishonour was not part of warfare.

Conversely, the wars in Central Asia were fierce struggles for survival, in which destroying the enemy and abducting their womenfolk were part of the scheme of things. Thus, when Mahmud of Ghazni's armies invaded India in 1000 AD, the burning, looting and massacre of civilians, along with the rape and abduction of women, was a culture shock to Indians. Kidnapping of women, forced marriages and concubinage then became prevalent, bringing to nought the code of chivalry and conduct prescribed by the kings of ancient India. In this battle of cultures, Indian society retreated within itself in order to protect its religion, culture and womenfolk from the barbaric onslaught.

Gradually the birth of a daughter came to be looked upon as unfortunate, as she was both a burden and a responsibility. In many parts of the country, a woman who repeatedly gave birth to daughters was despised or even discarded. Science had not progressed to the level it has today, in which it has been proved that the male bearing sperm is with the male. A daughter was regarded as *paraya dhan*, the wealth of her new family after marriage, who had to be protected at all costs, so that she could be handed over to her husband in a state of absolute purity. Purity and chastity became virtual obsessions. A girl's father could not breathe easily until he had sent off his daughter to her in-laws after puberty. Since everything was linked to religion, it was part of the father's *samskara* to marry off his daughter. If he fails to do so, there would be heavy penalties in his next life and considerable social approbation in the present one.

The uplift of women, their education and the need to banish *sati* and child marriage occupied the attention of all 19th century social reformers, such as Raja Ram Mohan Roy, Swami Dayanand Saraswati, Ishwar Chandra Vidyasagar, Swami Vivekananda and even Lord William Bentinck. Centuries of social segregation and suppression were sought to be undone, since they were a far cry from the glorious days of Maitreye and Gargi or even Razia Sultan and the Rani of Jhansi. The system of early marriage had led to the denial of education and, over a period of time, the situation was further compounded by the superstition that an educated woman was destined to become a widow! Despite all these efforts to uplift them, however, women in India remained mainly within the family, where they performed an endless cycle of gender obligations.

It was only after Mahatma Gandhi's entry into the national freedom struggle and his advocacy of women's rights that women emerged from the seclusion of their homes and into public life. As early as 1917, when Gandhiji visited Bihar due to the Champaran Movement, he had expressed his disapproval and opposition to the system of *purdah*. During the Civil Disobedience Movement, Gandhiji's call brought thousands of women onto the streets to face *lathis*, court arrest and fight shoulder to shoulder with men during the freedom struggle. Considerable leadership in this direction came from Swarup Rani Nehru, Vijayalakshmi Pandit and Sarojini Naidu.

When independence came, centuries of injustice was sought to be erased through suitable legislation and constitutional guarantees. The Indian Constitution barred gender discrimination and today, the Panchayat Bill allows 33% reservation for women. This ensures that, in principle, women at the rural and grassroots level have a say in the decision-making process.

Other Issues

Apart from constitutional provisions, there are other important issues that have a bearing on a woman's life and her activities. The right to abortion was given to Indian women in the early 1970s, although even today, in the United States, it is a burning and controversial issue. The termination of pregnancy, particularly at the teenage level, is done clandestinely and at high psychological and physical cost to the girl. In Ireland, a Roman Catholic country, neither abortion nor divorce is permissible even today!

It is quite evident, therefore, that despite being an ancient and conservative society, more has been done to secure equal rights for women in our country than in the so-called 'advanced' societies of the West. Women in India have access to the most advanced technical education, Constitutional provisions guard against gender discrimination and there is an effort to ensure equal work for equal pay, particularly in the realm of white-collar jobs.

Having discussed the historical compulsions of the past and the determined efforts to give the girl-child in India equal rights before the law, it is nevertheless important to examine the position of a girl in the family, as well as the attitude towards the birth of a daughter.

Whether Eve was created from Adam's rib or, as the legend goes, Brahma, the Creator forgot to create a woman and hence used many disparate elements in making her, women in all traditional societies were basically regarded as an appendage of men. This stemmed from the fact that societies were land- and war-oriented. Lands had to have male inheritors and so did thrones and titles. Frequent wars required men as warriors and thus began the great emphasis on the birth of a male child, so that family tradition and family honour could be protected. This orientation demanded the supply of an endless male lineage that would survive even when faced wth endless wars, disease and disablement.

A woman, therefore, had a place in society only as a helpmate to man in this endeavour. She was expected to produce a male child and the prestige of a woman depended on her ability to have sons.

The situation was no different in foreign lands. In the ancient city-state of Sparta, the Darwinian theory of survival of the fittest was carried to extreme lengths, where both weak and female progeny were flung to death from the top of a hill!

To some extent, this social abuse continues even today, as the girl-child in rural Rajasthan and rural Tamil Nadu are killed soon after birth by feeding her milk extracted from a poisonous plant. Using the advancement of technology, many practise female infanticide and abort the girl-child once amniocentesis reveals her existence. This moral issue is tackled at two levels. On the one hand, there are those who believe that it is better to abort a child rather than bring in an unwanted addition to an already burgeoning population. However, others feel pressured by the responsibility and economic burden of having girls in a society in which the dowry system flourishes, despite all the legislation against it.

Today, this selective abortion of the female child has resulted in an unfavourable population ratio of males to females, as revealed in the 2001 Census, particularly in the states of Punjab and Haryana. If the girl-child is aborted, who will give birth to the next generation?

Prevalent Attitudes
Towards the Girl-child

Half a century of independence, social transformation, media campaigns and education have undoubtedly had their effect on Indian society. Although in rural areas girls live under toil and subjugation even today, as they have for centuries, this is not evident across all levels of society, especially in urban areas. To some extent, the message of the small family norm, the spread of effective birth control methods, the benefits of education and the pace of development have all ensured a better lifestyle and more equitable spread of food, healthcare and education. Smaller land holdings and the mechanisation of farming have proved that a large family does not necessarily mean higher income generation.

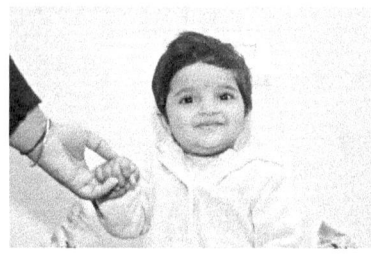

Across urban areas and smaller towns, lack of space makes it practical to have fewer children. Moreover, the fact that a significant percentage of girls are able to learn and earn, underlines the reality that a girl can also be an economic asset, rather than a liability.

In the higher-income groups, many married couples do not plan another child after the brth of the first child, irrespective of whether it is a boy or girl. Not only is the girl given the same education as a boy, but she is also encouraged to become a doctor, an engineer, a management or software professional or even a pilot or a member of the armed forces. In 21st century India, there is no area of any modern profession that is beyond the reach of a girl with the requisite qualifications, the determination to be what she aspires to be and family support.

Whereas, the 1950s and 1960s saw more women in their traditional role and less in the workforce, today, for any job, there are a large number of female applicants. In fact, one of the main problems girls and their parents currently face is the extent of commitment and dedication they extend to their careers, leading to postponement of marriage and the raising of children. Some hesitate to give up their economic independence for marriage, while others choose to be DINKs – Double Income No Kids – as they believe their career commitments are so fulfilling, there is no place in their lives to make the compromises that necessarily follow with the birth of a child.

The same mindset has found widespread support in the UK, where a poll conducted in June 2002 revealed that people felt children were an impediment to their professional progress, that they cost too much financially and emotionally and that they strained rather than cemented failing marriages.

However, DINKs are still not in a majority in this huge country of one billion population. Indian society remains deeply family-oriented, and Western individualism, freedom and affluence are not the overwhelming desire of the majority. Indian society realised much earlier what the West is realising today as a means of stabilising their crumbling society – a single person with a high income who has no one to return home to, soon feels insecure and lonely. It is this loneliness and insecurity that causes them to drift into casual relationships, drugs, alcohol or depression. In fact with their penchant for endless studies and research, they have now proved that those who are married, live longer!

Often, Indians go abroad so that they could send more from their huge earnings to their families back home. Despite affluence or social prominence, there is always a subtle pressure in Indian society on the individual to marry and settle down. Living alone by either man or woman is frowned upon, as people firmly believe that a single individual is incomplete unless there is a partner. This is particularly so with regard to daughters who, although earning well and soaring high in their careers, are a source of uneasiness to their families until they are married and 'settled' with one or two children.

Thus, even though the girl-child in India today has a more positive environment in terms of education and career opportunities, she is still made to feel that her role as a woman, too, must be fulfilled. This aspect is ingrained into her both by the family and society, so that she seeks to achieve a balance between her traditional role and career ambitions.

Whereas at one time both Western and Indian women resented being considered 'birth machines', today medical science has evidence of diseases that affect women who do not have children. Furthermore, the modern diet of junk food, alcohol, drugs and birth control pills play havoc with the female body and their effects on her are more lethal than on men.

Thus, while it would be untrue to say that the girl-child in India faces no discrimination today, it must also be admitted that in certain segments of society she is given the love, care, nurturing and opportunity she deserves. With characteristic Indian pragmatism, both parents and in-laws realise that an earning daughter or daughter-in-law is not to be frowned upon, particularly in view of inflation and the return on investment through education!

In more backward and impoverished communities, the birth of a second daughter may be greeted with gloom or forced smiles. In some backward rural communities, life for the girl-child may still be the same as what it was centuries ago. She is regarded as an economic burden on account of dowry, and as a security problem and a soft target that makes one vulnerable to enemies in the rough world of rural feuds. In many households, domestic duties are thrust upon her as early as when she is four or five years old, whereupon she washes dishes, looks after her siblings and is kept away from school. Diet-wise too, the choicest morsels are kept aside for the male child.

However, women-oriented social awareness programmes have now touched even the remotest parts of the country. The spread of education, television, rural development, immunisation, nutrition and literacy programmes have ensured that there is a perceptible change in attitude and the winds of change have ushered in new thinking, despite the gruesome figures of dowry deaths and female infanticide.

While the existence of dowry is lamentable and will be dealt with, in a later chapter, the problem of female infanticide, an unfortunate reality of our culture, has been heightened with the introduction of superior medical technology to have sex-selective abortions.

Historically, the frequency of war and the depletion of the male population through war placed a high premium on the male child. In all ancient and martial communities, therefore, the balance was heavily tilted towards the male. They would wage wars, inherit property and rule over kingdoms. The position of a woman depended on her ability to produce the all-important male child. Ancient India was a patriarchal society and in martial communities, such as the Rajputs, the frequent birth of a girl-child allowed the man to remarry so that he could beget a son.

The entry of women into the workforce and the post-World War constitutions that granted equal rights to women in most countries, including India, brought into sharp focus the position of women in society. In the post-sixties world of the emancipated woman, there is a new awareness of the extent to which women had been suppressed and, indeed, treated as second-class citizens in most societies, including those of the so-called advanced countries.

Today, statistics reveal that since more than 50 percent of marriages in the West end in divorce, there is a reduction in the number of united families, as against single-parent families, resulting in a negative population growth rate in Scandinavia, Europe, Russia and Japan. Thus, as society faces the problem of an ageing population that will soon outnumber the young, every birth is an important event and every baby a special. Maternal benefits are given to working women to persuade them that they will not lose out if they take time off to fulfil maternal obligations.

In direct contrast to these nations, ancient countries such as India and China face the problem of a burgeoning population, which is eating into the benefits of modern economic development. In earlier times, when healthcare was virtually non-existent and natural calamities and epidemics rampant, families provided for their future by having many children, as they knew that inevitably, only a few would survive into adulthood. In a predominantly agricultural society, numbers were required and children, sons in particular, were regarded as parental supports in their old age when they would no longer be able to work. Now, with improved healthcare and the spread of immunisation programmes to even remote villages, the rates of both infant and maternal mortality have fallen drastically and the chances of a child reaching adulthood are brighter. All these factors put together has resulted in the present population explosion.

When the Maoist Revolution overtook China, the Communist Government curbed the population by making the one-child norm compulsory. Traditionally, China like India, was a patriarchal society and women would secretly try for a second child in the hope of begetting a son. However, they would be coerced into having an abortion if they were discovered carrying a second child. Being a democracy, India is unable to use any coercive measures. In fact, the compulsory sterilisations carried out during the Emergency between 1975-77 set back the family planning programme due to the harshness with which the campaign was carried out.

India was one of the few countries to legalise abortions as early as 1970, so as to control the population by safely terminating unwanted pregnancies. Many view abortion as an ethical issue, which is why it has still not been legalised in many advanced countries, including the United States. In India, while abortion has been given moral sanction, the battle now rages against the age-old practice of female infanticide or 'gendercide', wherein, particularly in rural Tamil Nadu and Rajasthan, the unwanted girl-child is strangled, starved or poisoned to death.

With the typical Indian capacity to use modern technology to satisfy traditional requirements, amniocentesis (introduced in 1974 as a measure to ascertain congenital birth defects) was used by medical practitioners and parents for sex determination and sex-selective abortions. Many believed there were no ethical or moral issues involved, as the right to abortion condoned the taking of life, albeit only at a stage where the foetus was just a cell. Having accepted the right to abortion, why should the right to have a boy or a girl not be given and why should unwanted children be born, who would then be a burden both for the family as well as the country?

The evils of the dowry system make many communities in India consider the birth of a daughter a disaster, rather than as Lakshmi – the goddess of prosperity and wealth. In fact, the birth of a daughter signaled a life-long period of parental vulnerability, debt and humiliation. In urban and semi-urban areas, advertisements proclaimed the following: "Spend Rs 5,000 today and save Rs 5 lakh tomorrow", a pointer to the fact that female foeticide today would save a huge dowry in the future.

The 2001 Census figures shows there are only 933 females per 1,000 males. However, this is somewhat of an improvement over the 1991 figures of 927 females per 1,000 males. The marginal rise may be attributed to the literacy programmes, media awareness and the spread of healthcare and educational facilities. In 1901, however, there were 972 females per 1,000 males, since people did not have the 'advantage' of amniocentesis!

Despite glib justifications, a systematic depletion of one section of the population, the mothers of tomorrow, could not be allowed to thrive uncontrolled. The introduction of the Pre-natal Diagnostic Techniques (Prevention of Misuse) Act, 1994 was introduced by the Government to prevent 'gendercide'. The Supreme Court has put its might behind the implementation of the law. In one of its recent rulings, the SC took the State Governments as well as the Central Government to task for not initiating stern action against private clinics that have failed to register usage of ultrasound machines. In fact, the Court had asked

Health Secretaries and the Siemens Company to submit a list of clinics with ultrasound machines.

It is unfortunate that it required the Court's intervention for the Government to get cracking on such violators. Due to gender discrimination, 47 per cent of 15-year-old girls have a body weight of under 38 kilos and a height of less than 145 cm, both of which lead to high-risk during pregnancy. In addition, nearly 50 per cent of all women are anaemic. Hopefully, these statistics will gradually see a turnaround.

The Girl-child at Home

𝒶 child's first conscious memories are of its mother's arms, her voice, her warmth and the home. Even today, there are many joint families in India and the child grows up in the midst of an extended family where relatives, friends, servants and many other people drift in and out. A nuclear family or a single-parent household is still an exception in India. Indian babies are therefore quite friendly and do not shy away from strangers. Western children, on the other hand, have to be taken to the park or crèche so that they learn to socialise, as they frequently see no other person except their mother. Today children who are just about one year old are sent to school abroad so that they can play with and meet other children. Unfortunately, many working mothers in India too are following this trend and their sending children to playschools to 'meet' other children. Doctors do say that at this age the child's immune system is weak so infections are more easily picked up from other children.

Another malady that the Indian mother rarely suffers from, unlike her foreign counterpart, is post-natal depression, as Indian society views childbirth as a community, if not family, affair. The new mother inevitably receives a lot of help from family elders or experienced nannies, so that she is not overwhelmed by the magnitude of her new responsibilities as a mother,

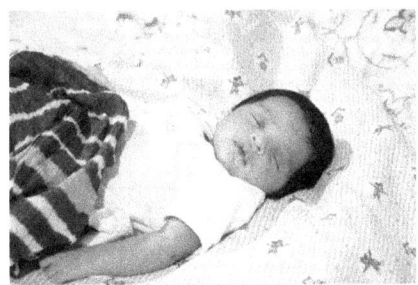

while still in a weak and vulnerable state after childbirth. In many communities, the new mother is not allowed to leave her room for a period of 40 days, so that she receives complete rest and a respite from domestic responsibilities. Once there is complete physical recovery, the chances of depression decreases.

On the other hand, the Western woman returns home with very little physical help. In addition, she is under pressure to regain her svelte figure and return to the workplace. Matters are even worse for the single, unwed or divorced mother.

As mentioned earlier, the birth of a girl-child in India is heralded differently in different families. While in some families she is greeted as Lakshmi, the goddess of wealth, in other households there are glum faces, especially if she is the second or third girl in succession. The girl-child is born a fragile and vulnerable entity. How her arrival is greeted and how she is nurtured and nourished plays a vital role in her psyche.

For example, the birth of Indira Nehru was said to be a disappointment for her paternal grandmother Swarup Rani, who was eagerly waithing for the birth of a grandson. Her grandfather Motilal Nehru, however, was highly accepting, which influenced Indira's attitudes in a very deep manner. Indira confessed to her friend and biographer that she overheard her aunt Vijayalakshmi Pandit referring to her as 'ugly' and 'stupid', which greatly scarred her at an age when she was both unsure and vulnerable. The end result was that she had an uneasy relationship with her aunt throughout her life. Her attitude towards her appearance and intellect was marked by insecurity which manifested itself in her hauteur and aloofness in later years towards those whom she perceived as better than herself.

Likewise, many girls are not really accepted because the family was expecting the birth of a son. Many do face these drawbacks and either cope with them stoically as the natural behaviour reserved for girls, or else they become cynical and strive to gain acceptance by being more assertive and aggressive.

In general, a girl-child has many different roles to play and many responsibilities to manage within the home. Her roles as daughter, granddaughter and sister are all essentially different from one another.

Relations with the Mother

It is rightly believed that a mother is a daughter's best friend and vice versa. This bond, which commences at birth and becomes stronger as the years go by, evolves in its own way at every stage of the girl-child's growth and development. Consciously and subconsciously, a daughter looks to her mother for guidance and support.

The first stage in the mother-daughter relationship is when the two- or three-year-old feels that her mother is a wonder woman. Irrespective of whether she is working or at home, the child is temporarily entranced by the abilities of her mother and starts imitating her in every conceivable way, from dress to speech, from the way she walks to the way in which she eats.

Unfortunately, this blind admiration undergoes some modification over the years. Sometimes, when the teenage years approach, this admiration may change to conflict, with the teenager feeling that she is not being understood or valued. At this delicate stage, when the girl is having a difficult time in coping with hormonal changes, the mother has to exert a great deal of caution and restraint, while giving unconditional love and support. The onus is on the mother, both as a mature parent and an older person, to guide the relationship in such a manner that unnecessary conflict and confrontation is avoided. Nature has made it such that a considerable amount of aggression is normal during the teenage years. However, if the parents adopt a consensual approach and are careful to keep their voices down and curtail the number of do's and don'ts, there will be a better response from the teenager.

When my elder daughter was a teenager, I was asked by a well known media personality who had split from her husband. "Do you fight with your children?" For a moment I was stunned. Why on earth should I fight with my daughter whom I loved dearly? It was an alien concept to me and one which I found to be below my dignity.

When I told her that I had no fights she said, "How do you manage?" The best way is to have a few issues on which one can have strict views and the rest can be resolved through discussion. For example, one may find that at this stage, under peer pressure and also due to a sense of independence, girls may turn clothes and make-up into an issue for confrontation. By continuously laying down rigid parameters on these issues, parents may create a situation in which unnecessary tension is generated. Sometimes, adopting a cool attitude helps. One simply overlooks or ignores the excesses as part of the folly of youth and pretty soon one would find that having elicited no response, the young return to accepted norms.

More often than not, the painful teenage 'you-don't-understand-me' phase can end smoothly if the mother shows maturity and also exhibits a lot of physical affection towards her troubled teenage daughter, who is struggling to come to terms with the visible and invisible changes in her body. It is the painful insecurity and lack of confidence in her appearance and the rapid changes in her body that trigger off unreasonable behaviour in teenaged girls. The necessary understanding and empathy is not always forthcoming from parents, which makes matters worse, for we should not, at this stage, try to find out what is wrong with our daughter.

Thus, during this vulnerable period of adolescence, the mother-daughter relationship can either be one of love, understanding and sympathy, which augers well for the future of the relationship, or it could be a time of bitterness, alienation and confrontation, which will blight future ties. This is a delicate phase, when the teenager thinks she knows best, that her independence must be respected and that she should be treated as an adult. Yet deep within, she is a vulnerable child-woman and mothers have to tread the fine line between a constant, domineering presence or absence and indifference, when all efforts to protect her daughter are rebuffed.

At this stage, the mother has to be like a friend, couching her advice and suggestions in a manner that will not be resented. Advice should be given more as guidance or by way of suggestion. A sense of responsibility should be subtly inculcated by placing great trust in the judgement and good sense of the teenager. By placing responsibility and trust, the teenager is made to feel adult and important, as these are higher emotions which call for a positive response, as opposed to a relationship in which the adults do policing and the teenagers play truant.

Once the teenager is convinced that things are not being imposed but suggested, they are usually more amenable. Guidance regarding dress, make-up, dealings with others, including the opposite sex, moral issues and the future role of the daughter as an individual, a member of society and as a woman can be given from time to time. It is only through love and affection that real respect and regard can develop, so that one is able to guide and influence the young. The earlier system of laying down the rules with a heavy hand no longer works in an era when peer pressure and other external influences, including those from the media and the Internet, are greater than at any other period in history. In order to cope with these external onslaughts, parents have to form an early and close bonding with their children, based on love and trust as well as respect, so that they can retain and influence them and mould their personalities and thinking.

Thus, there are many benefits of exercising restraint and tackling one's teenaged daughter in a manner that seeks her cooperation rather than her ire. By giving her space at this juncture, rather than playing an overbearing parent, one can avoid a lot of bitterness and steer the relationship towards a smooth future. You will know that you have achieved your goal and handled the situation maturely, when your daughter seeks your advice and values your opinion rather than oppose all that you say.

Around this time, it is also necessary for a mother to educate her daughter on matters of personal hygiene, beauty care and dealings with the opposite sex.

Towards the late teens and early twenties, the stormy years could end and the relationship can move ahead smoothly as one's daughter steps into womanhood. She is now a young lady with a personality and individuality of her own. Nevertheless, there is still a major role for the mother as she helps her daughter to tackle problems, some of which may occur at the workplace, while others are of an emotional nature, as she seeks relationships with the opposite sex or when the question of marriage arises.

When the daughter begins working, a mother must consciously detach herself and loosen her hold. At no stage should she exhibit any desire to share in her daughter's newly-found economic independence. One should accept graciously whatever the daughter gives by way of gifts, but one should covet nothing.

Once a daughter is married, even if she lives in the same city, one should make a determined effort to detach oneself and avoid interfering in the young couple's life, no matter how genuine the concern. It is only through non-interference that one can create a place for oneself as a repository of sage advice and moral support, if and when required and asked for. Depending on the amount of love or animosity the daughter has towards her mother, she looks upon her mother either as a role model or lives in dread of becoming like her. As per the category you fall into in the relationship with your daughter, you can gauge your success or lack of it in bringing up your daughter.

The New Pitfalls

The question of conflict with one's parents or child was virtually non-existent in the traditional hierarchical society of India, where roles of parents and children were clearly defined. There was no question of being rude or impertinent and not much importance was given to the child's whims and fancies.

With certain Western trends now creeping in and with peer pressures generating their own influence, some parents are taking their child's point of view into consideration, while others are bending backwards to appear 'hep' and 'with it'.

In their hearts, children look up to their parents as role models and expect them to behave in a conventional manner, without being unduly dominating and conservative. It is often a tightrope walk to achieve a balance between these two positions.

Give your daughter trust, space and privacy. Do not pry into her cupboard and desk or eavesdrop on her calls or conversations. Children will react better to trust rather than to suspicion.

A new and subtle area of conflict can be a mother's vanity and her obsession with looking good and looking young. Such conflicts are perceptible in America and other developed countries, where many a teenage daughter actually feels threatened by an attractive mother!

In our metropolitan cities too, the obsession with looking good has led to mother's striving to be attractive even when in their late 40s or 50s, resulting in a hitherto unknown phenomenon in Indian society – a mother who wants to be a 'teen-sensation'.Today, mothers and grandmothers are shedding their sari clad *avatars* and stepping out in jeans and capris, often looking better and more svelte than their teenaged daughter. Clinical psychologist Dr Ashima Puri explains, "Sharing and caring with authority is what the child's usual expectation from a parent-child relationship is. Even though parents would like to act young, some discrimination should be exercised. They should realise that their role involves a lot of maturity and understanding; they are seen as 'guides' and not as 'peers' to the child. Also there is the danger of an unconscious, underlying competition developing between the parent and the child."

Boys are as conservative as girls when it comes to their mother's wardrobe and dress sense. A 12-year-old boy told his mother, "Don't you dare step into school for the parent-teacher's meeting in jeans. If you want to come, wear a *salwar-kameez* or better still, a *saree*."

Avoid comparing your children to others, particularly unfavourably. As the adage goes, comparisons are indeed odious and children feel small and slighted when such comments are directed at them. Gauri hated it when her mother compared her unfavourably with her friends or cousins. When her mother asked her why she could not be like A or B, she would retort, "Why should I be like someone else? Am I asking you to be like their mothers?"

Many teenagers feel annoyed with their mothers when they say "No" without giving reasons, as the former feel they are old enough not to be dealt with in an arbitrary manner. It would be best to try and explain why one is objecting to something, rather than just laying down the law.

Relationship with Father

A study conducted between 1949 and 2001, published in the US in Review of General Psychology, December 2001, asserts that the degree of acceptance or rejection a child receives and perceives from his/her father appears to affect his/her development as deeply as the presence or absence of a mother's love. Parental withholding of love is connected to a child's lack of self-esteem, emotional instability, withdrawal, depression and anxiety. This increases the risk of developing problems with aggression, drug and alcohol abuse and delinquency.

In many cases, the study emphasises that the father's love is the sole determining factor when it comes to a child's problems with personality conduct, delinquency or substance abuse. Thus, while all may wax eloquent about maternal love, paternal love is also crucial to the child's development and well-being.

A girl's relationship with her father is of great importance as he is, literally, the first man in her life. This relationship will colour her relationship with the opposite sex in the years ahead. If he is dominating, distant and high-handed, she may either be attracted to a softer and gentler man or she may accept this dominance as the compulsory façade of all men. Often, a strict father faces a rebellious daughter and this determination to achieve on her own and not be under male dominance may influence her greatly.

Indira Gandhi's husband was the complete opposite of her father – a plebeian as opposed to the patrician Nehru – loud, hearty and a man of action rather than words, a person who worked with his hands rather than with pen and paper. The great English poetess Elizabeth Barrett Browning found her husband, Robert Browning, the complete opposite of her tyrannical father. The Orient too is full of heavy-handed dominating fathers who have regarded it their birthright to dominate their daughters' lives.

Daughters, therefore, sometimes have an awkward relationship with their father while their relation with their mother is warm. This is particularly so in traditional and conservative societies and especially where the father feels that the daughter must be kept 'under control'.

Do's and Don'ts for Fathers

- Fathers must not try to be too conservative, as it only fosters resentment and rebellion in their teenaged daughters. Times change with every generation and fathers must learn to move along with the times and stay informed on current trends: dress norms, age-appropriate behaviour, peer group pressure, socialising amongst girls and boys and the like.
- Be careful never to reprimand your daughter in the presence of her friends, irrespective of the misdemeanor committed; you can sound her out in private for a more responsive reaction.
- One must always keep the channel of communication open and understand one's daughter's point of view, as it is only then that one can exert real influence or elicit genuine cooperation. Control over one's anger and speech is essential when dealing with one's daughter. While the sight of a furious father will initially elicit fear, beyond a point this could finally turn into defiance.

Studies have confirmed that when a father is actively present in his daughter's life from her earliest moments, the bond that develops is close and lasting. As she goes through the trying teens, she looks to her parents to achieve the balance she often does not see in herself. She also looks up to her father as the source of adventure and action as he goes out and returns home with news of the outside world, particularly in traditional societies where the mother may not be working.

At this stage, a father can play a crucial role in building up his daughter's personality by fuelling her interests in different fields. If she is keen on swimming, he could be her first coach and if her interest were in the Milky Way, he could encourage her by taking her to the planetarium.

Considering this critical role, as a father you must:

- Never be violent when dealing with your daughter – unless you want her to hate you for life.

- Try to be a source of encouragement rather than criticism and discouragement.

- Couch all criticism with a degree of subtlety and gentleness.

- Be generous while paying her a compliment on a new dress, hairstyle or loss of weight, while at the same time retaining a sense of balance, which will not make her feel that life is only about external appearances.

- In selecting her life partner, allow her the power of veto. However, ensure you do not give her away to a person who has a long list of demands. In many cases that have resulted in dowry deaths, parents overstretched themselves simply to ensure a 'prestigious' alliance.

Relations with Siblings

One of the best parts of childhood is one's relationship with brothers and sisters. The bond of affection, mischief and living in a secret world different from adults forges ties that stretch into the future.

At one point, parents believe that the best way to encourage children was by stoking rivalry and competition between children. However, psychologists have now confirmed that this is least likely to achieve positive results. In every family there are some children who are more skilled, stronger or more talented than others. If undue attention and affection is given to such a child by the parents, not only does he or she become unduly proud and boastful, it also triggers off feelings of inferiority, inadequacy and resentment in others.

It is thus a primary parental responsibility to prepare the first child psychologically when a sibling is due so that the instincts of jealousy and anger, present in all children, are strictly within acceptable norms. The child should be made to feel responsible for looking after the new baby and given a lot of love and attention by the parents. Beware of others like relatives or friends, who make insensitive comments about the new arrival, as compared to the older child.

As the children grow, they should be encouraged to play together, share their room, clothes and toys. Parents should take care not to make the second child wear only 'hand-me-downs', but stitch new clothes for his/her birthday and festivals.

Do not make the mistake of always blaming the elder sibling for the mistakes made by the younger ones, as they will resent it. Also, parents should always talk to each other and their children politely and encourage the children to do the same. A low tone keeps emotions and language in check.

Maintaining Harmony

In other matters too, there should be a conscious effort on the part of parents to be fair towards all the children. For example, one child should not be sent to an expensive private school and the other to a local government school.

The same attitude should hold true when it comes to apportioning jewellery and garments between sisters. Also, if one has a son and a daughter or one son and two daughters, one should not go overboard in leaving the best for the son and his wife as upholders of the family name. As parents one should foster family unity and do nothing that is contrary to this.

Parents should be careful to have their immovable and movable property matters in order, well before they reach old age, as life is unpredictable and one must make a proper Will so that there is no unsavoury dispute later on. If there is no Will, the entire family, including brothers, sisters, parents and wife, have a share in this property.

Material possessions and property are the greatest source of domestic discord, despite all our spiritual pretensions. Thus, in the case of self-acquired property as well as jewellery, one should leave clear instructions to ensure the family's future peace and harmony.

Relations with Grandparents

As mentioned earlier, there is often more enthusiasm when a boy is born. This is sometimes made fairly evident by the paternal grandparents, who regard the daughter-in-law as the carrier of the next generation, which is possible only through the birth of a male child.

The gender bias is so rampant that a woman is blamed both for not producing children or for begetting girls, although science has long since proved that it is only the male who carries the Y-chromosome, which results in the birth of a boy. Men rarely get themselves tested for fertility as they and their parents are convinced that nothing could ever be wrong with them! All the blame is thus placed squarely and unfairly on the woman.

In too many such instances, the paternal grandmother then makes life miserable both for her grand daughter and daughter-in-law. In one instance, when 15-year-old Priyanka's mother was expecting a third child, she was told by her paternal grandmother that if her mother (whom she labelled a 'girl-producing machine') had a girl again, there was no reason for the 18-year-old marriage to continue! And this true story happened in the early 1990's!

A shocked Priyanka, who till then used to love her grandmother, kept this information to herself, as she was scared to upset her father by criticizing his mother and could not tell her expecting mother, who had already developed high blood pressure. Keeping these vicious comments bottled within herself, for the next six years she developed the most excruciatingly painful periods. Such malicious comments left, quite literally, a very painful scar.

Contrary to scientific studies, which confirm that the sex of the child is determined at conception, many mothers-in-law insist that elaborate *pujas* and eating of *prasad* after the third month ensure the birth of a male child!

However, the granddaughter-grandparent relationship can be an extremely sweet and mutually beneficial one, in which one generation catches up on the past, while the other is ushered into the contemporary world. The daughter must be told to listen to her grandparents with respect and patience. Unnecessarily arguing with them if they express a different point of view or answering back should not be permissible, no matter what the provocation.

Pitfalls Grandparents Should Avoid

In many households, three generations live under the same roof and grandparents are often very close to their grandchildren, loving, influencing and caring for them even more than the parents do. In such families there are no problems.

Difficulties arise when grandparents impose the standards and discipline of their generation and constantly pass critical comments. From making unwanted comments on their height, weight and appearance to snooping on their phone calls and curbing their outdoor activities, these prowling grandparents are so different from the traditional, benign and loving grandparents that their presence and conduct cause deep resentment and discord. If a grandparent has come on an extended visit, there should be an attempt at being close to the children. Adopting a critical attitude is the wrong approach.

Even as one forges a bond with the next generation and increases one's proximity to the children by being in close touch with them, grandparents should guard against certain pitfalls.

1. Grandparents are not substitutes for parents, hence they should appreciate their position and not seek to undermine the role of the mother and the father.
2. Do not interfere when parents are disciplining the child. An opinion that one has regarding the parent's behaviour should either not be voiced, or should be voiced when the children are not around. Children are born politicians and it does not take them long to sense discord and capitalise on it by playing one against the other.
3. Avoid rivalry. Refrain and restrain yourself from comparing your grandchildren either with their own brothers and sisters or with their cousins. Such comparisons are odious, counterproductive and undermine the child's confidence. All parents are sensitive and emotional about their children, especially today's parents. Unnecessary comments will alienate you from your children.
4. Avoid playing politics. Keep your rivalries, bias and vanity to yourself, by never asking the children about their 'other' grandparents or relations.

The Joy of Grandparents

"Grandchildren are in a way much more fun than one's own children, because you don't have the same feeling of responsibility. And also, having gone through the period of your own children, you know that children are much harder than you thought when you were very young parents." These were the sentiments expressed by Indira Gandhi, who had a tremendous bond of affection with her grandchildren.

The love and affection showered by grandparents on grandchildren has long been the stuff of folklore. Grandmother told exciting stories and cooked one's favourite foods. She offered unconditional love and refuge from the scolding of parents.

In India, grandparents are further distinguished by specific names, as against the blanket Western term "grandparent". The patriarchal side is called *Dada* and *Dadi*, while the matriarchal side is called *Nana* and *Nani*.

Tradition has it that *Nana* and *Nani* are even more indulgent towards their grandchildren than *Dada* and *Dadi*, though this may differ from family to family.

In earlier times, the newborn child was handed over to his or her grandmother, thus relieving the first-time mother of a great deal of anxiety and tension. C.J. Daswani, an eminent educator and UNESCO consultant, says that he and his wife never looked after their first two children, who were brought up entirely by his mother who lived with them. It was only when they had their third child that they mastered the finer points of child rearing.

Today on account of nuclear family patterns, particularly in urban areas, grandparents are not so closely involved in the upbringing of the new generation. However, working mothers the world over have realised the value of having their parents around so that they can keep a benevolent eye on children even if servants are present.

As with everything else, modern society has devalued human relationships and they are no longer what they used to be. Many independent minded and somewhat selfish grandparents do not want to be "dumped" with their grandchildren. They cite ill health, age, lack of space and so on for their inability to help out, but the underlying sentiment is more self-centred. Having brought up their own children and sacrificed for them, they do not want to be tied down to fresh commitments.

On the other hand, some working parents are also too demanding and expect their parents or in-laws to take charge of the children while they immerse themselves in their careers. Furthermore, they are ungrateful and dismissive of the help given by elders.

Another problem is that today grandmothers too are working. Consider the example of Mrs Sumeeta Banerji, a Programme Director with the Canadian Embassy in Delhi. Both her mother and mother-in-law have full-time jobs! Who helps out with her two small kids is a question of some jugglery, as all take leave by turns to look after the children when they are unwell.

What Grandparents Must Avoid

One set of grandchildren dreaded the arrival of their grandmother, the wife of an Army Officer, who had brought up her own children with military discipline. She would invariably come in with a long list of shortcomings on the part of the boys. She would try to discipline them, regulate their food and play, and supervise their studies.

Another grandmother decreed that her granddaughter was overweight, hence she would not allow her to add sugar to her tea!

Teenaged boys and girls are in need of constant reassurance, not critical comments, from their grandparents. Not surprisingly, both the children in the above cases dislike their grandmothers and have no desire to interact with them.

These instances emphasise the need for grandparents to be loving, non-judgmental and uncritical of grandchildren. Harshness and disciplining should mostly be left to the parents. Moreover, since many grandparents do not stay with their grandchildren, their arrival with a bagful of admonitions only causes a rift between the elders and the youngsters. Unwarranted carping and criticism strains what has traditionally been, in Indian society, a beautiful relationship between grandchildren and grandparents, so avoid this.

Do's and Don'ts for Grandchildren

1. Grandchildren must at all times be respectful to their elders, even in the face of admonishment and criticism. Any resentment that one may feel should be conveyed subtly and without being rude. Accepting criticism is part of the growing up process.

2. Try to be understanding and helpful. Frequently, elders are cranky on account of their ill health, so make allowances for this.

3. Try to include the grandparents in your activities and keep them abreast of what you are doing in school. Some schools, such as Delhi Public School, Vasant Vihar has a special day on which grandparents are invited to the school to be with the children and see their progress.

4. Grandparents are a storehouse of knowledge and experience, so spend time with them while they relate anecdotes about their lives and that of your parents.

5. 'Granny bashing' is a popular activity in England and, to some extent, in the US, where grandchildren make fun of their infirm and incontinent grandparents. Whatever their infirmities, these should never be made fun of, as just one illness or a few decades can reduce today's youngsters to the same condition. Television serials there make fun of elders on a routine basis, some of which are beamed here too via the cable network, this is part of the western obsession with youth. However, in our culture, age and white hair are traditionally given respect. Uphold our traditions. Keep it that way.

6. Old people also require a visible show of love and affection, so that they feel wanted. One can perform small tasks such as giving them their medicines, tea and food on time. It is reported that due to child abuse, neglect and divorce about four million children in the United States live in households headed by grandparents. Currently, the most famous grandchild to have been brought up by his grandmother is President Barack Obama, who lived with and was deeply influenced by his maternal grandmother.

7. Grandparents may suffer from problems like high blood pressure, anxiety, strokes and stress, part of which doctors link to the stress they face on being forced to play a parental role.

Most of the above problems can be avoided or minimised if grandchildren are taught to display a more accommodative attitude towards their grandparents.

Handling Teenagers

Adolescence marks a period of rapid and profound change in both the body and mind. Coping with adolescence and its attendant physical and psychological changes makes the teenage years a trying time for both parents and children. Children become more vocal about their opinions, their expectations and their desire for freedom. Often they adopt a collision path with elders, arguing and questioning until parents lose patience. I remember that one year our American fiend walked in and after some time said, "I have two teenagers in the house!," as though it were some calamity.

In fact, teenagers have an in-built desire to rebel and rail against any authoritarian stance adopted by parents. Being older in age and hopefully wiser – having passed through a similar stage themselves – parents should not only "play it cool", but also avoid reading out the riot act at every juncture. Avoid making too many rules and regulations. Above all, try to avoid rigid, unbending stances; these only foster rebellion.

This does not mean that parents should not exercise their judgement or lay down certain broad parameters of behaviour. In fact, teenagers expect that certain norms and standards be adhered to. Parents should adopt a pleasant and consensual approach to all matters rather than one of confrontation and expect blind obedience from their children. Times have changed and unquestioning obedience is something that vanished with the 19th century. Parents should lay down a few basic guidelines and ensure that these are adhered to, rather than make too many irritating regulations.

Teenagers require support, love and guidance from their parents but not constant policing. In fact, preparing your child to fly is part of the parenting cycle and this can be seen in the bird family and among four legged animals too. Therefore, by letting go gradually one would get a far better response if one dealt with teenagers like responsible adults, rather than irresponsible, unreliable juveniles. If one has built up a good rapport during the childhood years, the teenage years will certainly pass off more smoothly.

Traditional psychologists of the 19th century made out that the period of adolescence was marked by a period of dark, angry turmoil into adulthood. However, Dr Daniel Offer, an American psychiatrist, re-examined this concept of the teenage years during the 1960s and asserted that the idea that the teen years are necessarily a period of rebellion and madness has misled many.

During teenage years, family bickering increases due to issues like schoolwork, dress, friends, outings and household chores. A cogent explanation comes from the work of the Swiss psychologist Jean Piaget, who proved that children did not have the capacity for abstract and analytical thinking until the teenage years. It is the arrival of this capacity that enables them to question their parents' thinking.

An associate professor of education, psychology and pediatrics', Judith Smetana, contends that concentrating on the development of a child's ability to think logically is not useful in elucidating family relationships. According to her research, there are two fundamentally different worldviews at the core of family conflict. While adolescents tend to see much of their behaviour as a "personal" matter, affecting no one but themselves and therefore up to them entirely, their parents tend to stand for "conventional thinking", which sees society's rules and expectations as primary.

This dichotomy leads to commonplace clashes regarding dress, studies, cleanliness of the teenager's rooms and so on.

Smetana charts the thinking pattern of a teenager in the following manner. A child of 12 or 13 generally has little time for conventions when it comes to family issues. Between 14 and 16 years, the teenager realises that conventions are ways in which society regulates itself. Between 16 and 18 years there is again a period of rejecting conventions, but more thoughtfully. Between 18 and 25 years, conventions are once again seen as playing an admirable role in facilitating the business of society. This is why, usually, by the age of 15 or 16 years quarrelling subsides and is replaced by a period in which the family "negotiates" issues such as staying out late, going out with the opposite sex and so on.

Parents who try to exert too much control find it impossible to yield in a conflict where their teenaged children are trying to establish their own identities. In this trying period where teenagers try to express their individuality, even as they want to maintain a close and caring relationship with the parents, the parents have to be positive and caring in order to tide over this difficult period.

In cases where parents adopt the stance of being the last bastions of conservatism, or where they are harsh and judgmental, there is a great danger of alienation. When faced with a consistently negative and hostile environment at home, children will be driven towards their peer group. Peer pressure and camaraderie often lead towards anti-social behaviour, drug addiction, smoking, alcohol and sex. It is only through compassion, love, understanding and constant communication that parents can exert influence during this trying time of physical and psychological changes in young adults.

By giving the teenager some measure of freedom, privacy and respect as a young adult, parents may be in a better position to avoid teenage rebellion.

Some Handy Tips

1. Early bonding – the closer the relationship in the pre-teen years, the easier it is during the teenage years. Confidence and self-esteem should be built up by listening to them, so that they do not have to do outlandish things to gain your attention.

2. Share decision-making, as parenting does not mean being a dictator. By offering your child choices and including them in decisions, such as the decoration and cleanliness of their room and the like, it enables them to get a feeling of participation in the household.

3. Understand growing pains – don't exert your will over them for every trivial issue but keep a grip on the main ones. Do not peer over their shoulder at every stage but give them space and privacy.

4. Keep the lines of communication open on all topics, including sex, at all times. Make them a part of your lives by seeking their opinion regarding your clothes, make-up etc, so that they feel valued.

5. Make mealtimes a happy hour for family bonding and light conversation. Do not chastise them or broach unpleasant topics while eating.

6. Know your children's friends and encourage them to come over for meals occasionally or simply to drop in. Avoid harsh criticism of their friends. Peer pressure is a reality at this stage, as children around the age of 15 like what their friends are doing. The group that moves together does almost everything together, such as going out for movies or parties and liking the same music and film stars.

7. Set reasonable limits for going out, returning home after a party, going out for movies and studying. Adopt a balance between unrestrained behaviour and a jail warden's mindset. Share your worries with your teenaged children and convince them that your concern for them arises from love, not distrust. In this regard, the cellphone has become

an essential part of life. Avoid disturbing your children when they are out with their friends, but keep in touch through messages for convenience and their safety.

8. Remember your own teenaged years and understand that your child may take a bite of the forbidden fruit! See that accurate information about alcohol, drugs, sex and AIDS is given well in advance, through appropriate reading material and frank discussions.

9. Patience, understanding, love and compassion go a long way towards harmonious family relationships. Rocked by internal changes, your teenaged child needs this the most at the appropriate time. Remember this is a transitional phase and it won't last forever; so keep your cool.

Mistakes to Avoid

1. Do not be a control freak and monitor every minute of the child's day. I was recently shocked when a mother, who happens to be a teacher in a top Delhi school, told me that she had come to my house for lunch after locking her teenaged daughter in the house! She had also taken the precaution of locking the room where the TV and the computer/Internet connection was! As it is, teenagers crave for freedom. If they feel that their parents are like jail wardens they will be driven to escape this claustrophobic atmosphere. Children on whom unreasonable curbs are imposed thrive in rebelling against authority.

2. Avoid harsh criticism and a judgmental attitude. Teenagers are just learning how to cope with life – assist them, rather than damage their self-confidence with a carping, critical attitude.

3. Do not try to compete with them. The fact that there is a teenage child indicates you have grown older. Don't try to fight the years by dressing in tank tops and having a perm so that people ask, "Which college do you study in?" While today's society demands that everyone should look young and

fit, don't try to look and behave like a teenager and come into conflict with your teenage children who see a father or mother's attempt to dress and behave like them as a matter of embarrassment. There are other parents who are enrolling in social networking sites such as "Facebook" in order to keep an eye on their children, much to their chagrin.

Clinical psychologist Dr Ashima Puri asserts: "Sharing and caring with authority is what the child's usual expectation from a parent-child relationship is. Even though parents would like to act young, some discrimination should be exercised. They should realise that their role involves a lot of maturity and understanding. They are seen as 'guides' and not as 'peers'. Also, there is the danger of an unconscious, underlying competition developing between parent and child."

This is especially true when a mother is slim, good looking and sophisticated and her daughter is a plump, gauche and acne-faced 14-year-old. Adolescence is the time when children require the maximum guidance, but in a subtle manner. A boy would hate to be hugged in front of his friends for fear of being labelled 'Mama's boy'. At this time adults must behave like adults so that they can guide their teenaged children into adulthood. Most teenagers disapprove and are embarrassed by pony-tailed dads and mini-skirted moms who shriek, giggle and act like teeny-boppers!

In conclusion, given below are some points made by young adolescents of South Asia, who held a conference in 1998, during which they took out a document that recorded their opinions and feelings about the world around them.

Voices of the Adolescents of South Asia
Preamble

We adolescents are not only conscious of our rights but we also feel responsible for moving away from the "me" decade in which we are living, to a decade when adolescents will prove to be an important human resource for the betterment of the region. We pledge to make this a reality.

Our Perspectives

- We feel neglected, and so we need more attention, care and support from all.
- We feel we do not have the right to make our own choices, after knowing all the alternatives – choices relating to our careers, our friends, movements and life partners.
- We greatly lack proper and correct information and guidance, especially relating to our physiological and psychological changes.
- We are not allowed to express our emotions and ourselves.
- We are treated as immature persons. We desire to share responsibilities and prove ourselves.
- We are not given ample opportunities to ascertain our individuality.
- We feel that the dreams and aspirations of our parents should not be imposed on us.

Parents Can You Hear Us?

- We need you to listen to us – to our dreams, our experiences, our explanations, our insecurities and our achievements.
- Give us your time – you gave us life, now we want your time.
- Be our friends.
- Understand us.
- Don't hide things from us, especially when they are related to us.
- Give us the privacy and the space to grow.
- We prefer openness and encouragement to pressures and threats.

These were the emotions expressed by young people, not only from India, but also from neighbouring countries such as Nepal and Bangladesh, all of whom were from different socio-economic backgrounds. Parents would do well to keep these points in mind when dealing with their teenage daughters/sons.

Michael Jackson's song "They Don't Really Care About Us" is a virtual anthem for teenagers, most of whom, at some point or another feel alienated from their parents. Therefore give your teenager, who is a bundle of confusion, disturbed emotions and insecurity lots of love, time and understanding and harmony at home will be easy to maintain.

Educating Your Daughter

In the past, women's education became a casualty to social constraints. The situation is gradually changing. The female literacy rate that was 7.93% in 1951 has risen to 54.16% in the 2001 Census. This is indeed gratifying.

In educating a girl, one is improving the lot of the family, for the girl will be able to provide better health, hygiene and nutrition to the family. Her education can invigorate adult education in a joint family, bring down the rate of illiteracy, thereby stimulating educational consciousness and civic sense among family members. At the macro level, educating a girl leads to socio-economic development of the nation.

In ancient India education of girls had a significant place in society, but with the passage of time and changing circumstances, social evils such as *purdah* and the dowry system came in. When social reformers of the 19th century sought to revitalise Indian society and rescue it from the morass into which it had sunk, they all advocated women's education – right from Raja Ram Mohan Roy and Dayanand Saraswati to Sister Nivedita.

There are two aspects when one talks of education. The first pertains to academics and the basic skill of reading, writing and arithmetic. With the passage of a Bill that declares Education as a Fundamental Right, even the poorest of the poor girl-child in a remote village of this vast country will hopefully have access to some kind of education. Many state governments have special educational plans and programmes for the girl child in which school fees are waived and books and uniforms are provided in order to retain them in school. The *"Ladli"* scheme developed by the Delhi government is one such programme, as the girl child often has to opt out of going to school due to domestic work or lack of finance.

In elite sections of society, the education of a girl is being given equal importance and with the facilitation of student loans, even those not so well off can access higher education, including Medicine, Engineering and Management.

The other component of educating a daughter pertains to certain qualities that are valued in our culture, certain social etiquettes that she must be taught and her role as a transmitter of culture and tradition. Part of the education of a daughter also relates to her ability to dress appropriately, depending on the situation.

Early School Days

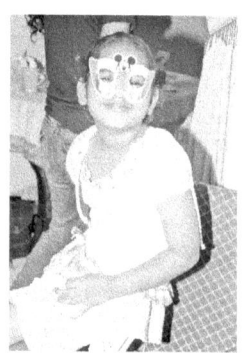

A girl-child is a big responsibility, as her safety is always a prime concern for parents. With a floating population of migrant workers, drug addicts, alcoholics, perverts and eve-teasers on the roads, instances of child abuse have been steadily on the rise. Thus all measures must be taken to safeguard your daughter. Unfortunately, she has to be protected even from relations and neighbours, who have been often guilty of child abuse.

- Be very careful about how your child goes to school, who picks her up and who drops her.
- If you pick her up and drop her yourself, it is fine. However, if someone else is entrusted with the job, s/he should be very reliable.
- If the child goes by school bus, she should be picked up promptly from the bus stand.

- Instruct the child never to go home with an unknown person, even if the person says that he has been sent by 'Mummy' or 'Daddy'.
- Teach your child never to accept any food and drink, including sweets, toffees or chocolates, from strangers.

The Middle Years (Between 10 and 17)

When your daughter is older, she is still innocent, but it is easier to explain things to her. She should be alerted to the fact that no one should be allowed to touch her body and that she should not remain alone with any male within the school premises. She should also be cautioned against eating from any particular vendor hawking outside the school premises everyday. It has been found that unscrupulous vendors sometimes lace their products with small amounts of drugs, which results in children unwittingly getting addicted to this.

It is only through loving bonds built up in early childhood that one can exert some influence over the child to counter peer pressure and other factors that assume importance during the growing years. A child should genuinely feel that her mother is her well-wisher and that she will receive understanding and sympathy, rather than admonition and disapproval, when she makes a mistake. One should remember one's own childhood and all the mischief one once indulged in! Moreover, every generation received disapproval from their elders for their ways and this trend will continue as long as humans exist.

Mothers should make it a point to be aware of their daughter's close friends, as they exert great influence at this stage. Encourage your daughter to bring her friends over from time to time so that you also get to know her group.

Children in middle and high school often want to bunk school and go out together for movies or an outing. Play along with this desire for some time and ensure that you know where they are going. If you can, give your daughter a cell phone for the duration of the outing so that you are in touch. Many children board the school bus, but go off with their friends, often from the opposite sex, before they reach school and parents are none the wiser. There is no foolproof method of monitoring one's children; hence the only way is to build up a reservoir of trust and common sense which would see them through the unstable years.

The College Days

If the school years were difficult, then the college years could be nightmarish for those parents who are unable to accept that their daughters are growing and have to be given some independence. This is particularly difficult for conservative fathers, who want to exercise absolute control.

One mother, sent away her only daughter to study outside their hometown as she knew that there would be unpleasant fireworks between her rebellious daughter and her conservative father on a daily basis – over her dress, friends, studies, partying and going out. She made this sacrifice at considerable cost to herself, but she rationalised that it would be better than having an unpleasant and violent scene on her hand everyday.

In fact, in India education is not the great leveller that it is expected to be. A man may be highly educated, but he carries with him his childhood values, standards and baggage. With economic advancement, one puts one's children in elite schools where they adopt new norms, but the father is unable to outgrow his childhood constraints. When he tries to impose these on his children, his attempts are met with resentment by the children who find him conservative and anachronistic.

Another pitfall of parenting in India, apart from overbearing supervision, is the tendency to lecture the young. In order to make up for long absences, parents – fathers in particular – feel that they are failing in their duty unless they harangue their children with advice whenever they meet. Children resent this and are non-receptive, so the entire purpose is lost.

While we do not want our children to be rudderless and excessively independent like in the West, where they may move out of the parental home at 16, there is no need to ram unnecessary advice down our children's throats, at a stage when they are trying to work out things for themselves and are particularly unreceptive.

The Hostel Years

Very often parents have no option but to send their children to other cities for higher studies. Some children go off at the school level itself, though this is not so common, as boarding schools have now become very expensive. At the school level, there is ample supervision, but the child does suffer from pangs of homesickness, craving for home food and the company of family members.

At the college or post-graduate level, institutional supervision is limited. Not all students get a seat in the hostel, so two or three friends may get together and rent a room, sharing the work and the expenses. Parents may help the child settle down initially, but ultimately there is no option but to leave the child on her own. One can only hope and pray that all the childhood bonding and indoctrination may now help theri daughter steer clear of drugs, smoking, drinking and promiscuous behaviour. Many children indulge in these activities purely to shock or to draw attention. A well-balanced child who was the recipient of a great deal of affection and attention will be less prone to indulge in these activities. At the same time, one has to be vigilant that the peer group does not lace some food or drink with drugs or alcohol in order to engineer a fall from grace.

As for indulging in promiscuous behaviour with the opposite sex, apart from the danger of disease, including AIDS, one should emphasise that the transience of superficial liaisons will only leave one with feelings of guilt, rejection and low self-esteem. One's body and mind cannot remain untouched by a casual sexual encounter or .relationship, hence one should be very judicious and mindful before indulging in physical relationships.

While on the subject of premarital sex, a recent survey revealed that the average age for losing one's virginity in India is around 23 years. This is heartening, as in Western countries, especially North America, those who do not shed their virginity by the mid-teens are panic-stricken! Yet in those countries there is a virgin movement which is growing, after having experimented with casual sex for many decades.

A Daughter's Socio-cultural and Sartorial Education

At one time, in most societies, including India, the primary concern with one's daughter was her marriage. Saving for her dowry, bringing her up correctly for the 'real' life at her *sasural* and ensuring that she looked beautiful were virtually an obsession with parents. Times have changed. Today, education is also given importance, but marriage nevertheless retains a predominant place in her upbringing.

In some families influenced by liberal Western thinking, there are efforts to bring up a daughter exactly as one would a son. This is particularly true of those families where there are no sons and the parents turn their daughters into substitute sons. Thus, you have daughters becoming engineers, police officers, pilots and so on. Today from spaceships to submarines and laboratories to stock-broking, the sky is literally no longer the limit for a woman in the professional world.

Despite her presence in the work sphere, the Indian woman has not lost her innate grace and become a hybrid species like her Western counterpart. An Indian girl still tries to combine her professional and domestic life in such a way that neither suffers. Many are staying home to nurture small children, then rejoining the workforce after the age of 40. Others are adjusting by starting lucrative ventures from home such as freelance writing, editing, home catering, chocolate making, running beauty parlours, crèches and so on.

However, problems may now be around the corner as globalisation brings in a new and compulsive work culture and obsessive consumerism, where status, pay packets and material possessions replace human values. Some couples are compromising by becoming DINKs – Double Income No Kids. Such couples are so absorbed in their profession and each other that they have no place for kids and a family in their lives.

Thanks to many such influences, there is a steady rise in divorce rates as women are no longer financially dependent on men and do not wish to languish in dead-end relationships. Tolerance, compromise and patience are at a low ebb. In particular, tolerance for the endless carping criticism of in-laws is at a very low ebb, with many marriages failing on account of interference from in-laws.

One can only hope that the next generation of 21st century daughters will not be dazzled by career options and including everything else. For those who miss out on the benefits of family life, there is a price to pay. Scientific findings confirm that if a woman does not fulfill her biological function of motherhood in time, she could be beset with all kinds of physical problems, including cancer.

Your Daughter at Home

Apart from school education, a mother has to involve her daughter in some other home activities. For example, during festivals you should instruct your daughter about religious and festive rituals, why they are performed and why she needs to participate.

You should teach your daughter the norms of Indian hospitality, which include making adequate food when guests are invited, ensuring that everyone has begun eating or has already eaten before the hostess commences and that all guests are made to feel welcome and comfortable. Besides, she should also know how to greet elders respectfully and make them feel at home when they come over.

Also, encourage your daughter to practice self-control in all matters – eating, shopping and acquiring.

For daughters who have studied and lived abroad, it is imperative to teach them Indian ground rules of entertaining friends and peers. For instance, if an American, European or Australian friend says, "Let's go out for lunch", it means that both will pay for their own meals. In India, however, the person who extends the invitation makes the payment.

If food is sent from someone else's house, the container is not returned empty but filled with some food item as well. If nothing is available at short notice, a bowl of sugar could be given in lieu.

As regards clothes, traditional dresses have been making way for bare-all, figure-hugging Western clothes. These dresses may be suitable for the disco or teenage parties, but are inappropriate at temples, *puja pandals* and even weddings – a fact parents should put across to their children. However, parents are sometimes so dazzled by the modernity of their offspring that they do not exercise their better judgement. But rather than having to impose a dress code for selected functions and festivals, it is preferable if the children are made to understand the importance of wearing or not wearing certain outfits.

A friend's daughter who is extremely fair chose to wear shorts on a visit to South India. Rural India is still highly conservative and people stared open-mouthed, wondering whether some film star or model had come on a visit. Such exposure in a rural environment is positively unsafe and inadvisable, particularly when visiting temples. One needs to dress appropriately, especially at places of worship.

In bringing up one's daughter, therefore, it is not enough to concentrate only on her academic qualifications. There is also the need to sensitize her to norms and traditions of acceptable social behaviour. While going to a disco demands a different dress code, so too one must dress according to the environment and occasion as a lot is determined by what one wears.

❀ ❀ ❀

Some New Hazards of Bringing Up a Daughter

Going back in time, it would be evident that families always regarded the upbringing and protection of a daughter as a problem. At one stage, a daughter was linked to family 'honour' in the West and *izzat* in the East, so she had no option but to tread the straight and narrow path to maintain the family name.

Today, rigid social divisions have crumbled across the world and individuals have greater freedom to pursue their own interests, desires and choices rather than merely fulfill family expectations. Urban living has given the individual a great degree of anonymity and privacy compared to rural living, where everyone knows everyone in the community and individuals are still expected to conform to set norms.

Despite the relative anonymity of urban living, people nevertheless build up their own relationships in which they and their children as well as their activities are known to others. As times change, however, so do the problems faced by people. Likewise, parents have to tackle a new set of problems while bringing up their daughters.

Case Study

It is really not advisable to do what my friend Usha, a teacher in a public school, does to her daughter, particularly when Usha goes out. Usha is determined that her daughter should excel in studies so that she can go abroad. Hence, when she has to go out, Usha ensures that rooms that have the phone, television, music system and the computer/ Internet are all locked! I was scandalised when I first heard this instance of utter lack of parental trust – that too by a teacher!

I was therefore curious to see the results of such strictness and was not surprised to find that Usha's daughter had a sour disposition and cribbing nature.

Today, as never before, the information explosion and the mass media have entered our lives in a way that simply cannot be wished away. Nor is it possible to isolate one's children from such influences. For example, the Internet can be accessed through a friend's computer or from cyber cafes. These new threats and external influences must be faced squarely and tackled, rather than being swept under the carpet by not having cable TV, a computer or Internet access. Children should be kept occupied with other activities rather than becoming couch potatoes.

However, children should be allowed some access to computers and the television, as all aspects of these modern amenities are not bad, particularly in terms of information dissemination and education. There are channels such as National Geographic, Animal Planet and Discovery that are very informative for children. Monitor what they see casually, not like some authoritarian dictator.

Boyfriends and the Opposite Sex

India has always been a conservative country and free mixing between the sexes has been restricted to certain echelons of society.

Girls' schools and colleges are located in every town in the country so that parents could enroll their daughters for education in a suitable environment, where she would be taught only by women and not have to intermingle with members of the opposite sex. As a girl's reputation precedes her to the in-laws' home, parents were reluctant to expose their daughter to the company of other young men, lest emotional and other complications spoil her reputation. Therefore, segregation in schools, colleges, hospitals, trains and buses has existed and still continues to exist in India.

Thus the concept of one's daughter having boyfriends, studying in a co-educational school or college and going on dates is still anathema to a majority of Indian parents. This is particularly true for school-going children. Part of the reservation stems from the fact that adults realise that during the vulnerable period of adolescence, children's emotions are raw and rarely balanced enough to deal with the ups and downs of a relationship, let alone with the opposite sex. It is the zeal to protect one's child from pain and suffering that leads parents to impose restrictions on mixing with the opposite sex. Considering the rising numbers seeking psychiatric help to tackle depression, low self-esteem, eating disorders and suicidal tendencies, one can appreciate and understand their position.

In the West, free mixing between the sexes commences quite early, even at nine or ten. Children often stay on their own once they are 16. Alone and insecure, half child and half adult, they are too proud to ask for help from their parents and thus look to relationships with the opposite sex as a source of affection and help. Earlier, Western parents too were strict and conservative and monitored adolescent relationships. However, changes in the social fabric and societal rules regarding romance, marriage, children and divorce have undergone a transformation so that adolescents no longer get that kind of protection abroad.

An Indian girl, on the other hand, is overprotected and cosseted. The extended family environment ensures there is no dearth of affection. Of late, however, experts have been shocked to find that

Indian children too are getting into relationships with the opposite sex as early as Class VIII. This means some begin experimenting around the age of 13 or 14, when they themselves are unsure where the relationship will lead.

Added to all this is the rosy image of love in the media, books, films, advertisements, and a narcissistic explosion of being obsessed with one's looks and figure, all of which leads to early sexual activity, abortions, emotional upheavals and unnecessary complications. Too much money, absence of parents from the house when the children return from school and a frivolous attitude are pushing youngsters onto this path, where they think everything is fine because they are in love. While boys may use love to get sex and girls use sex to get love, nowhere is this more evident than in adolescent relationships in which the old taboos have somewhat loosened and couples are going around and breaking up at the drop of a hat.

Eminent psychiatrist Dr Sanjay Chugh opines that sexual activity amongst school children has increased by as much as 500 per cent in recent years! "The major reasons are more openness in society, less hang-ups amongst kids themselves and, most importantly, the increase in stimulation provided to these kids by books, magazines and the Internet," says the Delhi-based psychiatrist.

Some parents frequently overlook these activities as they think they are 'cool' or 'liberal' in their outlook. But studies indicate that a female having a first-child abortion runs a five per cent risk of becoming sterile and being unable to conceive in the future. Furthermore, the stress and tension associated with clandestine sex may result in frigidity and many may not be able to have a normal sex life later on, due to diseases contracted through indiscriminate sexual activity.

The December 2001 issue of Reader's Digest has an interesting article entitled "A Parent's Guide to Teens and Sex". The article clearly advises parents to motivate their teenage children to delay sex by stressing on the moral dimension of sex, not just the physical and protective aspects, and then provide unconditional love and support so that they do not feel that sex is the only way to get this.

We would be failing in our duty as parents if, under the guise of being 'broadminded', we do not keep track of our daughter's interaction with members of the opposite sex and fail to provide her enough love, support and motivation to keep away from casual sexual relationships, which would undoubtedly have a scar on her mentally and physically.

Some Possible Solutions

- The channel of communication with one's children must be open and active at all times. No topic should be taboo and a mother should not hesitate to discuss issues like boyfriends, discos, partying and so on.

- At the school level, the child's attention should be on studies, sports and cultural activities.

- The attraction between young boys and girls should be tackled in a matter-of-fact manner. It should not be given the importance of being 'scandalous', as children are drawn like magnets towards forbidden fruit. It should be impressed upon one's daughter that it is better to wait until she is older before plunging into these complications and that there is more to life than attracting and seeking appreciation from the opposite sex. Moreover, by gaining a reputation of being 'available' and 'easy' she is unnecessarily becoming a target for abuse. One's body is something sacred and should not be used as a railway platform by casual acquaintances.

- At the college level, a girl may have a boyfriend and one should keep track of whom she is moving around with, as it is at this stage that smoking, alcohol and drugs are very alluring. One should try to see that one's daughter is with a group of friends rather than going on single dates, so as to avoid the perils of a relationship.

- Parents have to adopt a balanced approach when dealing with their daughter's mixing with the opposite sex. Extra strictness will only result in heightened 'boy craziness', while extra liberalism may have unpleasant consequences.

- The secret is to build up love, trust and self-esteem in your girl-child so that she herself is able to handle the interaction coolly and in a balanced way. Even in the 21st century there is no reason why your daughter should acquire a negative reputation or be called 'fast' or 'cheap'. The higher her self-esteem and self-confidence, the less prone will she be to compromise her dignity in any manner. Rather than making sleeping around a moral issue, it is more important to stress that one's body is something sacrosanct and others should not have easy access to it.

Valentine's Day

February 14th is celebrated as Valentine's Day all over the Western world. Valentine's Day is named after Saint Valentine, who was put to death on February 14, 269 AD in Rome. It is the day to celebrate love between couples, girlfriend and boyfriend or husband and wife. It is a day on which romance is celebrated and expressed through cards, flowers, chocolates and candlelight dinners.

Valentine's Day was virtually unknown in India a decade ago, until it came in through the flourishing greeting-card culture, a phenomenon which has taken over since globalisation began. While the Valentine concept is an imported one, it has a beneficial effect, as many Indian men are unable to express their feelings in a suave way – either they are reticent or they are crude and copy the antics of film heroes.

Seeing this public outpouring of love and romance on the streets, the Indian version of cultural policing has begun, with conservative groups trying to storm card shops to prevent the celebration of Valentine's Day, declaring it 'un-Indian'. Most people feel this is unfortunate, as it goes against the basic spirit of tolerance in the country. Celebrating Valentine's Day by merely exchanging cards or receiving a flower or bouquet from an admirer is harmless. Indian culture is too strong and deep-rooted to be shaken by one-day affairs like Valentine's Day. Love is a universal emotion and setting aside one day to celebrate it will make the world a better place to live in.

However, having said that, there is no doubt that Valentine's Day is an offshoot of globalisation, particularly in our urban centres. Such Western cultural influences are fine up to a point, but we should be careful to deal with the occasion in a balanced manner.

Dating

This is a recent phenomenon in the life of the Indian teenager. Unfortunately, the age at which it begins is getting lower and lower. It has long been a part of western culture, where it is part of the process of selecting a suitable partner. Today Indian children in Class VI and VII go on dates, sometimes with their parents' consent, but more often clandestinely. Such dates may mean eating together in the school canteen, sharing an ice-cream or pizza or even going out for a movie.

In America, there are two additional aspects to dating at a somewhat older age. One is going out on a blind date, which means going out for dinner or an outing with an unknown person. The second is the problem of date rape, in which a blind date can sometimes result in a violent encounter. An article published in the August 2001 issue of "Journal of the American Medical Association" reported that about one in five high school girls had been physically or sexually hurt by the dating partner. Not only was dating abuse ignored even in youth programmes, which were supposed to focus on problems like unwed pregnancies, addictions and their link to violence, but it was said to be a problem that occurred in all socio-economic categories.

While dating at the school level needs to be closely monitored, what with school- and college-goers frequenting 'afternoon discos', at the college level one will have to give one's daughter more freedom to go out with boys. However, parents should keep track and encourage children to go out in mixed groups rather than in exclusive duos. Sometimes a girl feels compelled to go out in a mixed group of girls and boys, so that she is not dubbed 'backward'. A certain amount of attraction and appreciation between the sexes is natural at this stage and this is what parents must keep in mind before laying down the rules.

Pornography and the Internet

The latest craze to hit young people worldwide, including India, is the Internet, e-mail and 'chatting' on the net. Many parents nag their children to stop talking on the phone and restrict their telephonic conversations with friends. Particularly where girls are concerned, parents are paranoid about boys calling and closely monitor the calls.

Today, however, children are simply using computers and the Internet to keep in touch. While parents may feel the urge to supervise this as well, making an issue of it will only result in children going out and using their friend's computer or those in a cyber cafe. Initially, all new gadgets have their own attraction and children will go on talking about them. But parents should not make any active efforts to curb this activity, as children will soon tire of it. However, any curbs at this stage will only make the child more attracted to the forbidden and they will do things clandestinely. Once the novelty has worn off, the child will then use the Internet primarily for e-mail.

A recent survey of youth aged between 15 and 24 years in the United States, published in "USA Today", revealed that they went online to procure sexual "health" information rather than to download music, play games or chat. These youngsters said they found the net important because they lacked "an already established relationship with a doctor; they want to do some exploring without anybody knowing about it", according to the author of the report, Victoria Rideout.

Another major danger is online pornography. Pornographic sites on the Internet have their own powerful attraction both for teenagers and others, particularly in view of our repressive and secretive attitude pertaining to sexual matters. Such sites will attract young people, despite parents' best efforts to ensure otherwise. In fact, the greater the mystery and secrecy regarding sexual matters, the greater the incentive on the part of the child to see and get information from these sites.

What Parents Can Do

If one is close to one's child one can openly discuss issues related to sex with her, so that the child can learn about the biological facts of life in a logical and matter-of-fact way and not seek clandestine sources of information.

Teenagers are always looking for information. They are eager to know about sex and hence they look to books, films and the Internet for information. Much of the information they receive surreptitiously is wrong or unscientific and this is where their problems begin – whom can they ask and how can they ask being the biggest ones. The information they generally seek pertains to conception and pregnancy, how to prevent it, what leads to Sexually Transmitted Diseases and what their symptoms are and whether masturbation is harmful or not.

Unfortunately, despite being the land of the "Kama Sutra", talking about sex has long been regarded as taboo in India, with the end result being that there is widespread ignorance. One should follow the advice of the celebrated authority, Kinsey, who said, "When parents sit on information that they should pass on to the child, the poor child starts wondering what is so secretive about it. His curiosity and interest are further increased. He begins either to think there is something shameful about his own body or he goes out to find the answers from friends. The eventual result in either case is usually bad."

Proper education is the only way to resolve this curiosity and parents, physicians and teachers have to play their role in this process. Parents must voluntarily tell children about the facts of life, as the more open parents are, the less curious and eager to experiment will children be. Proper books on sex education can be given to them so that their curiosity is satiated and their queries are answered.

The Tussle Over Television

Two or three generations ago, the bone of contention was going to the movies. Today the movies are in one's drawing room as television has virtually swamped our lives. Parents try to censor TV viewing and decide what the children can or cannot see. Some parents allow their children to watch only the Discovery and National Geographic channels.

By trying to control what your child should see on TV, one merely builds up resentment and since parents cannot always be physically present in the house, one only encourages them to watch what they want and not what you decree in your absence.

Parents are worried that their child will see something that they should not on TV, but it is not possible to protect one's child indefinitely. While one can restrict the hours that small children watch television so that they do not develop eye problems, one has to give older children greater freedom. One will gradually find that they themselves keep away from unsavoury programmes and have self-regulatory hours for watching television in-between sitting with their books.

Says an angry 14-year-old Sonal, "When my parents stop me from watching television I really get angry. After all, I know if my work is suffering or not. They don't need to keep reminding me about that."

Her friend Nisha is equally resentful: "If I am watching television my mother tells me how I could have utilised the time better by studying. It really irritates me."

One of the hazards of watching too much television – apart from eye strain and exposure to a surfeit of violence and noise – is that it leads to the couch potato syndrome wherein children plonk themselves before the idiot box, eat junk food and enjoy passive entertainment for hours on end.

Smoking, Drinking and Drugs

Indulging in smoking, drinking and taking drugs is considered a passport to adulthood. That is why, from an early age, children should be made aware of the hazards of these glamorised vices, so that by the time they grow up, they are suitably inured to their lure. Glamorous advertisements and the label of being 'modern' and 'smart' have begun luring girls from Class IX upwards into experimenting with these due to the encouragement from friends. What starts as social drinking or smoking at parties, in order to fit in with the group, soon turns into addiction.

Moreover, those girls who drink, smoke or take drugs are prone to many diseases, as they are affected by these sooner than men, whose bodies are better equipped to cope with the effects of alcohol and cigarettes. Medical research has confirmed that the ill effects of smoking and drinking affect the female body more acutely and swiftly than the male. Such girls also have more difficulty in conceiving, weight, growth and health are negatively affected.

One should be careful of the company one keeps. Sometimes, even if one does not want to booze, beverages are spiked with alcohol or drugs, making one an unwitting victim. At many parties, these methods are employed to drug the girl and molest her while she is in stupor.

Therefore, before allowing your daughter to go out for parties, ensure you know where she is going, with whom and whether you know anyone there. Also impose an appropriate curfew hour, by which time she must return home. Check her mode of transport. Rather than let her go with a group of rash drivers, when other friends are present, one could arrange for her to go in a hired taxi, so that she can return independently and within the prescribed time frame. At the school level, one could also limit the number of times she can go to parties every month.

Ultimately, how one's children cope with peer pressure and temptations that are all around is a combination of early childhood upbringing and their personal values. Parents have to instil such values in the child that even when she is exposed at the college level, she is still able to steer clear of vices.

Parents, on the other hand, have to be careful not to overdo or overreact while supervising their children. It has been found that children from the strictest and most conservative backgrounds are often the first victims of vice traps.

The Dangers of Consumerism

Traditionally, India has never had a consumerist culture and was more spiritually oriented. That is why, in the caste hierarchy, it was the man of prayers, learning and spirituality, the Brahmin, who was placed at the top of the social hierarchy, followed by the warrior-king, the Kshatriya, after which came the man of business.

Today, we are no longer able to resist the worldwide consumerist culture and have, in fact, joined it with gusto. One indicator in this regard are bride burning and dowry deaths, which still occur at regular intervals even in a city like Delhi. Statistics show that there were 13,612 dowry deaths reported in the country in 1998-99, with 6,637 brides burnt in 1999. There may be hundreds of cases that have gone unreported. We have become slaves to our possessions and consumerism is pushing us into needlessly multiplying our needs.

We have to plan our lives and train our children in such a way that we are not consumed by consumerism. It has rightly been said that the mad scramble for wealth and material possessions is as depressing as poverty.

The dividing line between a man's need and his greed is a very fine one, so unless we train ourselves to retain our balance and be content within our means, we will needlessly ruin our lives and become unhappy. Parents should be frank with their children regarding their economic status and financial commitments and not try to live beyond their means.

We should teach children the virtues and satisfaction that come from living honestly within one's means. If parents, particularly the mother, do not go on grumbling about all that they cannot afford to buy or do on the present income, then the children too will not be attracted towards an inflated lifestyle or envy their wealthy friends.

One of the unfortunate trends of modern urban life in big cities is that there is too much illicit money floating around and many ignorant parents are giving their children huge sums to spend in hotels with their friends. They are even given cars to drive, often when they are not licensed to do so.

At the college level, if not earlier in schools, such boys wish to attract friends, particularly girls, by taking them for meals to five-star hotels, to discos and so on. I remember, when I was in college nearly three decades ago, there were certain groups of fast girls who would willingly go out with boys/older men to hotels and allow their escorts certain liberties, in return for dinner at a five-star hotel or restaurant! Thus it would not be true to assert that morals have plummeted only in this generation – such things also happened in the past.

Mothers must caution their daughters against being taken in by the glib talk of wealthy boys, who can lure them to farmhouse parties and take liberties. The need to always maintain dignity and self-restraint and not be dazzled by wealth should always be underlined.

Discos, Clubs and Parties

At a certain level of affluence, particularly in urban centres, teenagers have access to discos, clubs and parties. The young have a great deal of energy, are naturally outgoing and gregarious. They often get together to celebrate birthdays, the end of exams and so on. Such celebrations and mixing on a periodic basis are quite acceptable.

The problem arises when unsavoury elements creep in and introduce drugs, drinks or start taking liberties with the girls. At recognised clubs and discos there is strict monitoring of entrants and the staff are vigilant about any public misconduct. The danger occurs when one's daughter is going to such parties in someone else's car, who may be an unlicensed, rash or drunken driver. When these parties are organised at private residences or farmhouses, certain dangers are present.

Since one would not like one's daughter to be a paranoid social recluse, one can send her to these gatherings occasionally after duly cautioning her about the perils involved. She must enjoy her youth, freedom and carefree life during the last years in school and initial years in college but parents can always give a few words of advice. A certain deadline for returning home may be imposed after mutual discussion. Any delay should be conveyed to the parents, so that there is no unnecessary worry and tension.

A Daughter's Physical and Mental Well-being

As a mother, your daughter's physical and mental well-being is always your primary concern. Having a daughter is an even bigger responsibility for a mother, as you will soon realise that you alone are her real well-wisher and protector in a world in which sometimes even family members are hostile to her existence. Thus the major onus of loving, cherishing and protecting a girl falls on the mother, who would gain manifold in the future for the initial years of unconditional love. A daughter's lifelong devotion and commitment to her parents is something that is being increasingly acknowledged even by those who yearn for sons or already have them. In many instances which are visible in the society in which we live, parents or widowed mothers often prefer to be with their daughters rather than with their sons and daughters-in-law, as the bonding with daughters is closer and there is greater empathy/sympathy.

The bond between a mother and daughter may be tested to its limits at times, but learning to understand each other's changing needs can bring you closer than ever. The mother-daughter relationship is also unique for its reciprocity, for what one does and feels inevitably affects the other.

I remember when I gave birth to my first child, a daughter, after the initial feelings of joy at having given birth to a perfectly formed, beautiful girl, one of the thoughts that went through my mind was that I now had someone to whom I could give all my jewellery! While some may feel this was an inane thought, it was nevertheless what I felt at that time, and underlines the psychological feeling which a woman has towards her daughter.

When a mother looks at her baby daughter, she sees herself as she was and when the baby gazes back at her, she catches a glimpse of what she would become. From the little girl who walks and talks like her mother to the rebellious adolescent testing the limits of her mother's love and patience, the umbilical chord between a mother and her daughter is rarely cut. It is the desire to protect one's daughter that often causes conflict, particularly at the adolescent stage.

Physical Well-being

Traditionally, Indian mothers and grandmothers have paid great attention to massaging and bathing the baby, applying kajal to the eyes and so on. In fact, there are certain professionally skilled women who are employed to take care of the new-born child and the mother, so that the latter regains strength fast.

While Westernised doctors scoff at these traditional methods and even caution that putting *kajal* in the child's eye could be harmful, there is no reason to disregard these traditions. The problem with *kajal* arises when commercial preparations are used, some of which contain lead. However, the traditional one was made at home with lampblack, everyday, so there was no question of contamination.

The child can be gently massaged prior to being bathed and bow-legs straightened out in the long run. A gentle oil massage benefits the infant. This has been underlined in the book "Child Care by Dr Suraj Gupte", who says that giving the "baby a gentle massage with olive oil, coconut oil, mustard oil or any other proprietary baby oil, before he takes bath will help to keep his skin soft and healthy".

Thus the physical care of a daughter commences as soon as she is born and mothers take great pride in seeing her bloom. The physical care of a daughter should only be handled by the mother, a senior lady in the family or a female servant. Never entrust a male servant to bathe your daughter, change her nappies or wash her. Unfortunately, child abuse is a global reality and male servants are one of the chief offenders. Always keep your daughter clothed and even when she is very young, do not dress her in frocks that are too skimpy. A girl-child may suddenly put on weight or start showing some bodily changes, in preparation for puberty, as early as the age of eight or nine. So ensure that she does not wear very tight or short clothes at this stage. Her genuine innocence at this age makes her a soft target for paedophiles.

A girl-child should receive proper nourishment, so that she is able to produce healthy children when the time comes. This is why the growing trend of girls as young as 12 and 13 going on a diet is a threat to their future health. Correct body weight and proper nourishment are very important components during pregnancy. An underweight woman is likely to have more difficulty in conceiving.

In looking after the physical well-being of a daughter, one should not encourage the use of pencil heels from a very young age. These shoes cause the body to be poised at a very odd angle, which strains both the spine and the uterus, one of the many reasons why Western women are plagued by excruciating backaches during and after pregnancy. These women also tend to miscarry and experts have often pointed fingers at high-heeled shoes. Wedge or block heels are much safer for young girls.

Preventing Child Abuse

Of late there has been an alarming increase in cases of child rape, molestation and abuse. Technological advancement has been employed for this purpose, particularly abroad. Paedophiles and other perverts are logging onto certain web sites on the Internet and indulging in child pornography and related aberrations. The Internet and cell phones are a boon for adults who prey on young people for sex. Paedophiles have gravitated towards the Internet because it offers anonymity, immediate contact with children and the facility for storing photographs.

UNICEF figures estimate that about one million youth under the age of 18 are forced into the sex trade annually. India too is no exception to this trend. Both girls and boys are at risk. Worldwide studies confirm that one out of four children go through such abominable violence. Recently there was a horrific report from Bhopal, shown on television, in which a 16-year-old girl escaped from her father's clutches and reported to the police that she was the mother of a one-year-old boy, a product of their incestuous relationship! A three-year-old girl was raped by her father in Netaji Nagar, New Delhi and succumbed to her injuries.

These incidents merely confirm what author Pinkie Virani's book, "Bitter Chocolate", asserts – 20 per cent of boys and girls below 16 years in India are susceptible to child abuse. Fifty per cent of those being abused at home are victims of adults known to them. Thus, there are big bad wolves in every home and since about 71 per cent of the child abusers are family members or friends, no action is taken against them.

Records show that there is a shocking 30 per cent rise in the rape of minors, many of whom are kidnapped, raped and then killed. These were the findings of Pratinidhi, an NGO working actively with minors, especially around Delhi. Many teenagers were lured by neighbours or close relatives. Most of these rapists had easy access to the house and no previous police record. While the parents did not suspect them, the victims were often too young to understand the intentions of the rapists and were taken by surprise.

Tips to Protect Your Daughter

- Parents should not allow young children to either go to the neighbours unescorted or allow male neighbours to come in when the children are alone. Says Roli Sud, Campaign Manager of Save the Children (a UK-based organisation whose Calcutta chapter organised a meeting on child abuse in India in December 2001), "About 71 per cent of child abuse is committed by family members or friends. So most families don't take action."

- Children need to be warned not to trust strangers. The male child is as vulnerable to child abuse as his sister.

- They should be warned never to accept chocolates, foodstuffs or beverages from unknown or little-known people.

- If anyone tries to molest or tease them, they should not hesitate to tell their parents. There is nothing to be shy about or hide. In fact, those who indulge in child abuse count on the fact that the child would be too shy or frightened to complain.

- Keep a sharp watch over all male relations, cousins and their friends. None should be allowed access to the house when the children are alone.

- Be very cautious before employing a male servant. Many young males from other states come to the big cities in search of white-collar jobs, but are often reduced to taking up domestic work. One such servant boy from Orissa stole a picture of my friend's daughter and sent it to his village, saying it was his of office girlfriend! When she intercepted the letter, my friend had no hesitation in throwing the boy out before he caused further damage.

- Be extremely careful about your daughter's tutor. Make sure you are always around when he comes, that your daughter is decently dressed and not sitting too close to him while studying. If possible, it is better to employ a lady tutor for your daughter.

The recent case in which a tutor allegedly pushed his student to her death from the terrace is a case in point. In September 2001, Delhi tutor Ravi Ghai allegedly pushed his student (with whom he was purportedly having an affair) from the fourth floor, resulting in her death.

Renowned psychologist Dr Aruna Broota of Delhi University says that hero worship of a tutor of the opposite sex can lead a girl to have a crush on him, particularly since he may be helping her in a subject she finds difficult. While Ravi claimed that his student was in love with him and wanted to marry him, and his refusal to do so led her to commit suicide, eyewitnesses however told the police that they saw Ravi pushing the girl to her death.

Recently, newspapers mentioned that students had complained about noted *Kathak guru* Ram Mohan Mishra making "obscene gestures" and "overtures" towards his students who were in the 9-12 age group.

Eve-teasing has been somewhat glorified in our films, hence the average man, who may be otherwise timid or repressed, feels emboldened to act as the heroes do in films. Today, things are going too far. Thwarted, jilted or jealous lovers are kidnapping, raping, throwing acid or even murdering the objects of their 'affection', hence warn your daughter that casual encounters are fraught with risk in a society in which too many people are on a short fuse and cannot handle rejection from a woman!

The Right Diet

Obsessed by the 'thin-is-in' syndrome, many of our metropolitan hospitals are getting a new range of patients who are as young as 11 years. Recently, the Psychiatric Ward at the All India Institute of Medical Sciences, Delhi, had two 11-year-old patients suffering from anorexia nervosa, who had been admitted because their obsession to lose weight was so acute that they not only lost weight, but also muscle and essential body fluids, leading to severe dehydration. One of the girls weighed as little as 17 kg. Such girls rubbish parental concerns and chew on carrot sticks, which is simply not enough to sustain growth.

Experts warn that the media focus on pencil-thin models, an increasing and unhealthy obsession with one's looks and body image, and the zeal to wear figure-hugging clothes and attract boys will lead to increased eating disorders such as anorexia and bulimia in the years ahead. With slimming centres mushrooming and potions and machines assuring a 'perfect figure' over the counter, people have not yet realised that quick weight-loss programmes damage the liver, kidneys and heart in the long run. Teenagers are willing to skip meals in the hope of shedding weight but they still gorge on junk food and alternate between fasting and feasting.

Fast foods such as pizzas, burgers and French fries add to empty calories, as they have little nutritional value.

A balanced nutritious diet is essential during the crucial growing years. Lack of essential nutrients, including a chemical called serotonin, leads to depression, a common affliction amongst teenagers. Excessive starvation could lead to hormonal and chemical imbalance and thyroid problems.

Even girls from affluent families are said to be suffering from malnutrition. What is the reason for this terrible malady and what can be done? An eminent endocrinologist says, "We are gripped by the look-thin mania. Girls of families where a good figure, dieting and exercise are prevalent are easy prey. Mothers want to look better and be taken for their daughter's sister and the latter does not like it."

Thus an obsessive, narcissistic vanity and the media, which glorifies the emaciated Twiggy or Kate Moss look, is playing havoc with our physical and mental health. Everyone is looking for shortcuts – losing weight without exercising, starving but not cutting out the empty calories of junk food and showing a complete lack of balance when reducing weight.

Parents must be careful so that their harsh or insensitive comments regarding their daughter's appearance does not trigger an eating disorder, the after-effects of which can be lifelong. One of the side effects of stress, loss or gain of weight, anaemia and excessive exercise is amenorrhoea – the stoppage of menstruation. Patients of anorexia and bulimia are highly susceptible to this. An eminent gynaecologist reveals the reason for this: "Their body weight is too low to sustain a pregnancy and such women often experience amenorrhoea. The reproductive system shuts down as a sound security alarm."

Precautionary Measures

- As a mother, build up your child's self-confidence and self-esteem. Be careful about her diet from childhood, interspersing nutritious meals with the occasional 'fun' or junk food. If pizzas, hamburgers and *samosas* are totally banned, the children will have a burning desire to consume them, which is not the aim of this exercise.
- Make sure that your daughter exercises, play games, learns yoga or takes up Indian or Western dance.
- Make her aware of the value of balanced meals, fruits and vegetables, as well as dried fruits and nuts.
- Inculcate higher values and interests in her, which allow her to go beyond physical appearances and an obsession with her figure.
- Convince her through your talks that people who gravitate towards someone only on account of their looks or figure are not worth cultivating.
- Do not talk about models, beauty queens and film stars as role models of success and fame, nor express awe at the amount they earn. Daughters are often unconsciously pushed into trying to fulfill their mother's ambitions.

I was shocked while talking to a young mother in her mid-forties recently, who said that she could not bond with her second daughter as she was 'too fat'! I was utterly shocked and scandalized, being of the opinion tliat a mother's love was unwavering and unconditional. I cautioned her that such feelings would immediaitely be felt by her daughter who would never forgive her if she knew this.

Clothes and Make-up

Make the selection of your daughter's clothes a joint effort from an early age so that during the crucial teenage years there is less conflict on what is appropriate dressing. Allow her freedom in small matters, so that on the bigger issues your better judgement prevails through subtle control.

Explain to her that in India, the selection of clothes sends its own signals and dressing soberly has its benefits. For instance, unemployed youth and men loaf around at market places ogling girls and their figure-hugging clothes. Why make oneself the object of their lewd discussion? Tell her that appropriate dressing for the occasion is essential, so bolder or Western outfits should be worn for places where they are acceptable, such as friends' parties or discos.

As for make-up, the glow of youth calls for a light hand when using cosmetics so that one's natural beauty is highlighted.

The Right Values and Attitudes

It has rightly been said that the hand that rocks the cradle rules the world. A mother is the child's first teacher and role model. At one time, Sita, Sati and Savitri were the ideals of Indian womanhood. Integrity, virtue, sacrifice, consideration for others, tolerance and self-control were the ideals to be followed.

Today, with a vengeance, daughters and other women are being exhorted to fight for their rights, grab what they can, pull the right strings, make the right connections and get ahead. While standing up for one's rights is fine, one should not think that success at any cost is the ideal. The means to the end should be above board and not at the cost of personal compromises. If women retained their integrity, so would the family.

- Teach your daughter the path of moderation, self-control and contentment. Teach her to laugh and be happy.
- Happiness and material wealth are not really linked, for if they were, depression, substance abuse and addictions would not plague Western society.

- Consumerism and material success must be kept in perspective and some detachment exercised over all this.
- It is very important to encourage your daughter to cultivate a sunny temperament and a positive outlook, for when she is married and the lady of the house, her moods can make or mar the household.

Impatient, attention-seeking, immodest, selfish and inhospitable – these are some of the characteristics that young girls of the 1990s and the 21st century are cultivating, duly encouraged by their over-ambitious mothers, eager to fulfill their own suppressed desires through educated daughters. Such women will not be able to hold families together or bring up decent children and our society too will witness the hollow decay of the West.

Rather, one should strive to achieve what Indian society has done over the centuries – a fusion of that which is the best of both the East and West.

Mental Well-being

Growing children are highly self-conscious and vulnerable, with a tendency to wilt under criticism and thrive when praised. A mother wields enormous influence over her children, which is enhanced if she is balanced in her approach and judicious in her choice of words. Sometimes, careless remarks and harsh criticism can scar a person for life, as in the case of Indira Gandhi. There are other instances, too.

Bani was the typical old-style mother, making scathing comments about real and perceived flaws in her children, thereby scarring them for life with her harsh words. She told her daughter Priti that she should not smile in photographs as, when she did so, an inordinate amount of gums showed. The end result is that Priti is stiff, unnatural and unsmiling when being photographed.

My cousin Priya, who lives in England, is married and has two daughters. While her elder daughter was always frail and uninterested in eating, the younger daughter seemed to have a real weakness for food, particularly sweets. Since living there means wearing Western clothes, my cousin was very particular that the children should not develop an 'Indian figure'. Once when she caught her younger daughter eating cake with icing, she beat her and made her spit it out! Since then, the girl is very reserved in her mother's presence, looks at her mother with resentment, has turned cranky and dreams only of food.

Cases like these illustrate the point that parents should be extra sensitive when it comes to criticising or correcting their teenage daughters. Since adolescence marks the time when the teenager is finding her own individuality and trying to fly on her own, mothers should exercise self-control and exhibit unconditional love and compassion, rather than make scathing and hurtful comments.

This age is such that violent mood swings, feelings of inferiority and depression are some of the mental states in which an adolescent may find herself. Hormonal changes are one of the causes of mood swings, while undue self-absorption can lead to feelings of inferiority and an unbalanced diet may give rise to depression.

Depression

Around the age of 13 or when they reach adolescence, young girls tend to be prone to depression, which is a disturbed state of mind. They stop talking to those around them, even their friends and siblings, do not mix with anyone, do not go out and retreat into a world of isolation and loneliness. This has become fairly commonplace on account of working mothers, many of whom are not able to devote sufficient time to their children. Some teenagers are into having boyfriends at a very young age, smoking and drinking, even taking drugs and tranquillisers, all of which can have a negative effect on their mind.

Depression may also be triggered by feelings of inferiority vis-à-vis siblings or friends, lack of confidence and self-esteem and other related factors. Any of these factors or a combination of them may lead a girl to feel low, running herself down and hesitating to talk to anyone about her feelings.

Some Tips

Parents must tackle their child's depression at the earliest. The moment they see their daughter retreating into a shell, they should spend as much time with her as possible and give her constant reassurance.

Talk to her and try to get to the root of the problem. Encourage and support her to boost her confidence. Do not allow her to be alone for long periods. Be with her, offer compliments and talk about the positive aspects in her personality.

Involve her in activities that will keep her occupied, going so far as to gift her a pet, if she so desires.

Parents can tide over this phase, which may have well been triggered by their callous conduct, by exercising the utmost tact, patience and understanding. In short, exercise restraint when dealing with your teenaged daughter during her troubled phase.

A leading psychiatrist in Kolkata is alarmed at the rise in child psychiatric patients in the city. A study has revealed that extreme stress both at home and in school is increasingly causing "acute depression" in children. Compared to two or three cases a few years ago, presently at least 12 children go in for counselling every month. Strangely enough, all the children are from good schools where they are overworked and treated shabbily. Psychiatrists attribute bad parenting as one of the leading causes of depression, suicidal tendencies, mood swings, stress, sleep disorders and the neglected-child syndrome.

Today's crèches, where children are dumped by their working parents, do more harm than good and the physical and mental abuse that the child is subjected to here adds to the problem.

Reducing the Causes

The pressure to perform in school is one of the major reasons for the steep rise in child psychiatric cases. The solution lies in better parenting, family support and attention at home. Children should be given an adequate diet, vitamin supplements and rest, along with a flexible routine. They should not be made to rush from school to tutors or for extra sports and music lessons. A disturbed child should be given counselling if the parents are unable to cope.

Inferiority Complex

Due to heightened emotions and acute sensitivity, adolescents sometimes experience feelings of inferiority vis-à-vis others. As they take everything very seriously and to heart, parents should be careful before making any caustic remarks, as these can instantly trigger feelings of inferiority in your daughter. This may also occur if there is a better looking, more talented and outgoing sibling, making the other child feel inferior.

Feelings of inferiority can also develop with regard to one's friends, particularly a pretty friend who attracts all the boys, a rich friend or a more popular and brilliant friend.

Fortunately, like many other factors during adolescence, such an inferiority complex can also be a passing phase, which subsides after the girl develops her own personality and self-confidence. Prior to this, she may develop a very defensive attitude towards everybody, is always on guard against comments made by anyone and can be fairly short-tempered. In extreme cases, she may even cease to talk to her friends or parents.

Helpful Tips

- If the inferiority complex has stemmed because of careless comments from parents, they should make a conscious effort not to hurt the child further.

- Where a sibling is the cause of the complex, parents should emphasise that both are equally talented, brilliant or good looking in their own way. This would boost your daughter's self-esteem and help her shed her feelings of inadequacy.

- When the complex is because of her friend's circle, ask your daughter to change her group, make new friends and move around with those who are more like her. Explain to her that she should be comfortable with her friends and if she is not, then there is no point in having such friends.

- If the complex stems from the fact that her friends are more studious, parents should stress on the fact that she too can do. In fact, most problems arise because parents are always quick to make unfavourable comparisons with their child and others, often taunting them as to why they cannot be more like their friends.

- Sometimes teenagers cover their feelings of inferiority by living in a make-believe world and presenting a picture of themselves and their background that is far removed from reality. This is particularly true when they perceive that their parents are not as rich or hep as those in their peer group.

Increasingly, on account of the influence of television and beauty pageants, undue importance is being placed on one's appearance. Dr Achal Bhagat, a Delhi-based psychiatrist, says that one of the reasons for the alienation and rejection of teenagers from their peers stems from their appearance. "Success is more important now and how you look often determines your success," she says.

However, parents should stress to their children that beauty is only skin deep. And besides, with a proper dress and make-up sense, it is always possible for a girl to look more attractive than she actually is.

The Role of Physical Fitness

𝒫hysical fitness is extremely important once your daughter gets into her teens. This is the time when youngsters use their pocket money to gorge on junk food. With visuals of junk food being splashed over the pages of dailies or being aired on TV, thanks to aggressive advertising campaigns by McDonalds, Pizza Hut, Wimpy's and the like, teenagers think it's the in-thing to be feeding on junk food or downing morsels with Coke and Pepsi, rather than a glass of water. It is not long before excess weight begins creeping in on their waistlines.

Pizzas, burgers, French fries, pastries and other such items have nothing whatsoever to recommend them, except empty calories. Besides burning a hole in teenage pockets, such fat, oil and sugar-rich foods can lead to multiple ailments in the long run. Is it any wonder that youth in their 20s are now falling victim to early-onset (juvenile) diabetes and end up having to monitor their insulin levels every single day?

It is also not surprising to see young children's teeth chequered with cavities, thanks to the harmful habit of guzzling colas every other day, if not everyday.

Many parents complain that their children are no longer within their control and despite admonitions, continue feeding on junk food and colas. In many cases, the parents are themselves to blame, as they too are addicted to such stuff! It becomes difficult to restrain the kids when you cannot restrain yourself. If this happens to be your problem, rather than preaching what you yourself cannot practise, it would make more sense if you took some preventive measures to balance unsavoury eating habits.

The best option in such circumstances is regular exercise to keep one's body fighting fit. There are many options available and you could choose one that suits you and your teenage daughter. The options include walking, jogging, aerobics, cycling, swimming, yoga, etc. We shall, however, discuss the options purely from the angle of your teenage daughter.

Walking: This is possibly the best and safest of all options. If there is any public park near your neighbourhood, an early morning 20-to-30-minute walk five or six times a week has excellent health benefits. It keeps one's tummy in check, controls fat levels, improves stamina and endurance, besides having a host of other benefits associated with all forms of exercise. You could use canvas shoes or sandals for walking – whatever you are comfortable with.

The amount of calories you burn per day through this form of exercise will depend on your walking speed and the total time spent (for total calories burnt, see the Calorie Chart). Experts recommend that one alternate between a fast and moderate speed. That is, walk at a moderate pace for five or ten minutes; then a fast pace for five or ten minutes; then again at a moderate pace. However, if you are more comfortable walking at a specific pace only, do just that.

You could also spend some time walking barefoot on grass, which is considered to have more therapeutic benefits, as it directly stimulates various nerves connected to the soles of the feet. The best thing about walking is that there are no harmful effects whatsoever.

Calorie Chart
(Calories burnt in various activities)

	Activity	Cal. expenditure per minute
1.	Laying still	1.0
2.	Sitting, standing, reading, writing,	1.5
3.	Driving a car, tailoring	2.0
4.	Washing floors, sweeping and ironing	2.2
5.	Golf	2.5
6.	Walking @ 5 km per hour	3.0
7.	Walking @ 7 km per hour	4.5
8.	Walking @ 9 km per hour	9.0
9.	Gardening, weeding etc	5.0
10.	Cycling (depending upon speed)	3.5 to 8.0
11.	Boxing, rowing	12.0
12.	Dancing	5.0
13.	Table tennis	5.5
14.	Tennis	6.0
15.	Swimming @ 3 km per hour	9.0
16.	Football	8.0
17.	Running (depending upon speed)	10 to 25
18.	Other exercises:	
	a) Light	2.5
	b) Moderate	4.0
	c) Heavy	8.0

Jogging: Those looking for a more strenuous form of exercise could consider jogging. Like walking, this too is best done in the early morning hours. It is best to use canvas or sports shoes for this purpose. Besides, as far as possible, it is safer to jog over a grass or sand track, rather than a concrete surface. Jogging over a concrete surface could lead to shin and joint problems in the long run.

You could burn up a lot more calories through jogging than walking. Having said that, however, be warned that jogging is a high-impact activity that could lead to some problems. For instance, a regular early morning jog without properly warming up could lead to swelling of the feet. So, before getting into your stride, ensure at least half an hour of walking and other activities to get the blood flowing after a long night's sleep.

The other bad effect some people report is that over a sustained period of time, jogging makes one look haggard. So, despite the extra calories it burns vis-à-vis walking, jogging may not be the best option for your daughter on a regular basis.

Aerobics: Literally, the word aerobic denotes "with oxygen" or "in the presence of oxygen". Aerobic exercise is any activity that uses large muscle groups, which can be done continuously for a long period of time and is rhythmic in nature. Aerobics helps the heart, lungs and cardiovascular system process and deliver oxygen more quickly and efficiently to every part of the body. As the heart muscle becomes stronger and more efficient, a larger amount of blood is pumped with each stroke. This means that fewer strokes are required to rapidly transport oxygen to all parts of the body. An aerobically fit individual can work longer, more vigorously and achieve a quicker recovery at the end of each aerobic session.

Like all forms of exercise, it has multiple health benefits. However, like jogging, many aerobic exercises include high-impact movements that could lead to injuries, if not done under proper supervision and after warming up adequately. In fact, jogging itself is a form of aerobic activity. Ensure your daughter practises aerobics under a qualified trainer and performs the warm-up and cool-down exercises, the latter being as important as the former in preventing soreness and injury.

Another way out is to practise low-impact aerobics, where one does movements without jumping and jarring the rest of the body.

Cycling: An excellent way to increase endurance and keep fit. Cycling at 20 km per hour is a good way to work up a sweat. However, it is the muscles of the lower body that are directly exercised.

Swimming: This is the only form of exercise that ensures a workout for almost the entire body, including the eyes. But one must never swim on a full stomach, as this increases the risk of a heart attack. A light snack is allowed, however, especially if you are swimming in a river. This is because if one swallows some contaminated water accidentally, it lowers the risk of paratyphoid. This risk is not present in chlorinated swimming pools, though.

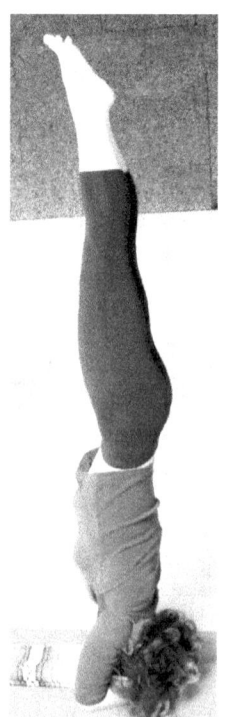

The downside on swimming is that it leads to a marked darkening of the skin. However, the skin gradually returns to its normal colour once swimming is discontinued. All in all, it is one of the best forms of exercise.

Yoga: The world's best, most comprehensive system of exercise, yoga has innumerable benefits. It cures, controls or prevents anxiety, asthma, arthritis, blood pressure, back pain, chronic fatigue, depression, diabetes, epilepsy, headaches, heart disease and a host of other ailments. Of course, your daughter wouldn't be having these diseases at such a young age! However, there would be other direct benefits for her, as yoga:

- Improves muscle tone, flexibility, strength and stamina
- Lowers fat
- Stimulates the immune system
- Reduces stress and tension
- Boosts self-esteem
- Improves concentration and creativity
- Improves circulation
- Creates a sense of well-being and calm.

Do bear in mind though, that yoga should be practiced under the guidance of a trained person, as there could be harmful effects if it is done incorrectly.

These are just some of the popular forms of exercise that we have outlined. There are other forms of exercise too, especially sports, which could ensure your daughter stays fit as a fiddle. If your daughter is the sports-loving kind, she could indulge herself at the school, college or residential sports club. Badminton, lawn tennis, table tennis, volleyball and cricket are just some of the games that could ensure a good workout for your daughter.

A note of caution! If your daughter has not been exercising before, she should initially restrict the duration to just 20 minutes, irrespective of the form of exercise. After a couple of weeks, the duration could be gradually raised, when her body is used to exercising. During the workout session, if there is any feeling of discomfort or pain, she should take a break immediately and rest for a while. Exercise is not recommended during periods of illness. She could, however, exercise during her menses if it doesn't cause her any extra discomfort. In fact, her menses would be less painful, problematic or prolonged if she exercises regularly.

Do also ensure that she wears loose, comfortable clothes while working out, preferably cotton, since it absorbs sweat better than synthetic garments.

Remember – there is no better way to prevent disease and retard ageing than exercise.

With fitness being part of what is regarded as 'beauty', women are working out not only to look and feel better, but also to develop endurance, energy and stamina as they challenge male domains. As they sculpt their bodies to keep pace with their demanding lives, many are turning to yoga to combat the aches and pains which result from sitting for hours before their computer. Professional life is highly competitive, hence one has to be in good health in order to be part of the race. Thus, a balanced diet and a correct balance of rest, exercise and some vitamin supplements will stand your daughter in good stead in the years ahead when she balances her life as a wife, a mother and a professional.

Emotional Well-being

When your daughter enters the teens, one of the most important factors that will stand her in good stead throughout her personal and professional life is her emotional strength and well-being. Being emotionally resilient can make all the difference between winning and losing. It can also make the impossible possible.

But this will not happen all by itself. The right emotions also have to be fostered and fine-tuned, just the way one would do with one's body to ensure its well-being. It is very important for your daughter to know how and when to express her emotions. And how and when to refrain from expressing her emotions and controlling them, instead. All this is a fine art, though, which will take time in mastering.

The teenage years are a time when girls are likely to fall in and out of love! Sometimes at the drop of a hat! This is natural and nothing for you to be alarmed about. Which is not to say that you don't take precautionary measures. To begin with, it is necessary for you to make your daughter understand the difference between love and infatuation. The emotion that a young girl most often feels for her teacher or professor is nothing but infatuation, a passing teenage crush. At this stage, though, your daughter will be convinced this is the real thing – this is her Mr Right. Except for the object of her affection, nothing else may seemingly matter.

Mother's Guile

This is the time for you to use all your guile and play it cool. Openly trying to dissuade her from this infatuation – which is what it is, you realise with all your hard-boiled experience – will be counterproductive. The more you try to pull her away, the more strongly will she be attracted to the man. Rather than ticking her off for the crush, you would be better off seemingly teaching her some "tricks of the trade" and making her think you are on "her side"! So play along.

The first thing she should be told is that she must never ever wear her heart on her sleeve. Tell your daughter that making her affection clear to the man (or boy, as the case may be) will only make her seem so "gettable", "approachable" and "cheap". The charm of a girl lies in her inaccessibility and unavailability. For this, she has to play hard-to-get – even if that's the last thing she's feeling.

Such a shrewd tactic on your part has many benefits. Firstly, if the man hasn't already sensed your daughter has a crush on him (he probably may have already cottoned onto her feelings!), it makes the chances of him realising this, thereafter, all the more difficult.

Secondly, it introduces the element of time, thwarting or delaying the chances of anything happening between your daughter and her supposed "heart throb". There's nothing like playing for time in such situations. More often than not, she may simply outgrow the infatuation over the days, weeks or months. She may suddenly realise that she no longer "loves" that guy, but is actually in love with Aamir or Shah Rukh Khan! Which would be all for the better, as these film stars wouldn't pose a threat to your peace of mind or your daughter's chastity!

Thirdly, even if the guy reciprocates her "love", the chances of the affair taking off immediately are somewhat dim. Don't forget – the smart mother that you are, you have taught your daughter how to play hard-to-get! This again buys you more time to add some other spoke in the love wheel; of course, without your daughter getting wise to what you are up to. Remember – you are on "her side"! These lessons ensure no Romeo will be able to easily take advantage of her naiveté and take your daughter for a ride.

If things do not go your way, however, and your daughter is involved with some Tom, Dick or Harry teaching her to be emotionally resilient is still important. More often than not, such affairs fizzle out before long, with the girls left jilted and nursing broken hearts. If this happens with your daughter, this may seem like the end of the road, and the world, for her.

You know it is not! You have to quickly convey this very fact to her. And lot's more… A boy who has jilted her is not worth the tears and heartache she is putting herself through. There are many other fish in the sea – better ones at that. All that happens, happens for the best. Any guy who deserted her didn't deserve her in the first place! Finally, she is really lucky that a jerk like this guy is no longer in her life, because he wasn't the right person for her anyway. Mr Right has yet to arrive. And so on.

By constantly reinforcing her spirits with positive thoughts, you will help your daughter hold herself together and pull through emotionally. At such delicate moments in life, it is control of the mind that matters. If she can manage this, she will always be her own master (mistress if you please!). This will also ensure she does not slip into a slough of despondance or despair, nor flirt with a nervous breakdown. At her age, that's the last thing she should be flirting with, anyway!

Emotional resilience is not just important for her personal life. It can make all the difference between success and failure in the professional sphere too. An emotionally strong person is better able to command respect, win support from peers and colleagues, motivate better performance from herself and subordinates and achieve excellence in her professional life.

Expressing Oneself

Of course, make it clear to your daughter that being emotionally tough and resilient does not mean that one should not express one's feelings in weaker moments, pretending one is hard as nails. Such an attempt to bottle up emotions will be futile and counterproductive.

There will be moments in life when your daughter feels low and there may or may not be any valid or apparent reason for this. At such times, she may feel like simply bursting into tears. Tell her to go right ahead! More often than not, the spontaneous release of tears tends to have a cathartic effect. When something is wrong, trying to suppress her emotions will only lead to problems, physical as well as mental, later on. In such a scenario, it is better your daughter cries and unburdens herself, rather than pretends everything is hunky-dory. Of course, she is better off doing this in the confines of her home or room.

Inculcating such a pragmatic attitude in her will also ensure that she is comfortable in sharing her problems with you, since she knows you will not berate her for "shedding useless tears". So, while emotional resilience would require her to be smart and not expose her feelings to all and sundry, at home she should discuss her ups and downs with you. For you don't just have to be her mother, you also have to be your daughter's good friend, if not her best friend. Once she feels you stand by her through thick and thin, she will feel emotionally secure through all phases of her life, good, bad or indifferent.

In short, your daughter should be taught that in life one has to maintain a healthy balance between emotion and rational thought. There may be times when one has to go by what the brain says. At other times, one has to listen to one's heart. Maintaining this fine balance is an art. But once you stress the importance of this and give her the necessary guidelines, she will ultimately learn when to follow her head – and when to follow her heart… not her heartthrob!

Handling Puberty and its Problems

$\mathcal{P}$uberty is the most tumultuous period of hormonal change in girls and boys. It is a time of tremendous emotional, physical and mental upheaval and requires a concerted effort on the part of the mother and daughter to get through the period as a normal phase of life. Generally, adolescence starts when the individual attains sexual maturity and ends when independence from parental authority is assured. Since the age of sexual maturing varies, it is difficult to delineate the period of adolescence.

Adolescence refers to all stages of maturing, while puberty relates to sexual maturing only. While the period of adolescence may be said to be between 14 and 18 years for boys and 13 to 18 years for girls, puberty is an overlapping period. Out of an average of four years, about two are spent in preparing for the body reproduction (this period overlaps the end of childhood, the so-called pre-adolescence and pubescence). The remaining two years are spent in completing the process. To know what the hormonal changes entail, one needs to understand the complex process that goes on in the adolescent body.

The Physical Changes

For most girls the development of breasts is the first physical sign of puberty. However, for some girls it is the appearance of pubic hair that heralds puberty. The development of breasts is stimulated by ovarian activity and the production of the hormone, oestrogen. For this to occur, the area in the brain called the hypothalamus has to mature and send out steady hormone messages to the pituitary gland in the brain. This, in turn, has to produce enough FSH (Follicle Stimulating Hormone) to get the follicles present in the ovaries to develop and produce oestrogen.

Besides, oestrogen also promotes fat accumulation in the hips, thighs and buttocks, so that body curves appear. It also changes and thickens the vaginal wall, causes the uterus to mature and grow and also the cervix to produce mucous. This results in a light yellow tinged discharge and many confuse it with an infection. Some adolescent girls are so horrified with this that they start hiding their panties in shame and suffer psychological trauma.

Just before, or about the same time, a second group of hormones produced by the adrenal glands are pushed into production by the hypothalamus and pituitary glands. These are the male-like hormones called DHEA and androstenedione. They stimulate growth of pubic hair, followed by hair in the underarms. The testosterone-like qualities of these hormones also cause girls to develop acne, perspire and acquire body odour.

Most often, adolescent girls who suffer from body odour develop an inferiority complex and use all kinds of cosmetic products to overcome the odour. An intelligent mother should be able to instill a sense of security in her daughter by pointing out that it is a natural outcome of being a teenager. The emergence of acne also disturbs the teenager and the mother could alleviate her concerns by being supportive and trying various herbal methods to combat the problem.

This phase, activated by the adrenals, is called the adrenarche. Incidentally, these male hormones are also responsible for developing sexual interest of girls in males. Meanwhile, a third hormonal upheaval occurs simultaneously. It is the increased production of growth hormone, which interacts with many other crucial hormones such as insulin, thyroid, adrenal and sex hormones, causing a spurt in growth of bones and organs. During this spurt, height increases about three and a half inches each year and this usually continues from the beginning of breast development until the onset of periods. Once the menstrual cycles are regular, most girls add just two or more inches to their height and stop growing between the ages of 16 and 18.

As girls grow taller and their body fat nearly doubles, they gain an average of seven to nine kilos over a two-to-three-year period. This is generally known as puppy fat, which normally sheds by itself in a few years. Sometimes, this spurt in body weight can also have psychological effects in an adolescent daughter. She has to be reassured that it is a passing phase.

The last major physical sign of puberty is menarche, or the first period. The follicles in the ovaries finally reach maturity. Both the hormones, oestrogen and progesterone, are released and cause the uterine lining to become thick and after two weeks, if no pregnancy occurs, the hormone level drops and the lining sheds. This is the first period. Once it starts, however, this complicated hormonal system may still have inconsistencies. So periods are often irregular for the first two years after menarche.

With changes in dietary habits and other environmental factors, the average age of menarche has reduced greatly in the past decade. Some girls have their menarche at a comparatively early age and is called precocious puberty. A child may suffer from anxiety because her peers have not begun menstruating. This is a crucial period and the mother has to act as a counsellor and guide to her daughter by explaining that it is quite normal and nothing to get upset about.

On the other hand, some girls have late menarche. Although the age for menarche can vary from 11 to 15, some girls who do not menstruate till late feel quite troubled since most of their friends are in the stage of menarche. In such cases, a mother should counsel and reassure her that it is normal for a variation in the age group to occur. Consulting a doctor could also reassure the teenager.

A teenaged girl will also be worried about the state of her skin during this time. The skin may get oilier and pimples could appear. It is important to clean the skin and use a deodorant or antiperspirant on underarms to keep odour and wetness under control.

Despite best efforts, pimples will keep appearing because of hormonal changes.

Emotional Changes

In addition to the many physical changes that occur during puberty, there are many emotional changes as well. The teenager may start to care more about what other people think about her and would want to be accepted and liked. At this time, relationships with others may begin to change. Some become more important and others less so. The adolescent begins to move away from the parents and identify with others of her age. She may begin to take decisions that could affect the rest of her life.

Many girls of adolescent age feel self-conscious about their changing appearances – too tall, too short, too fat, or too skinny. Because puberty causes so many changes, it is hard not to compare what is going on with one's body to what is happening to one's friends' bodies. The mother has to repeatedly assure the daughter that everyone goes through puberty differently and, eventually, everyone catches up.

The insecurity and uncertainties that hound an adolescent may not appear very serious to adults, but for them it is a very serious matter. Gentle counselling and guidance at every stage could help the adolescent emerge with a healthy attitude about the entire process.

This is also the time that sex education becomes imperative and mothers should warn the child about the hazards of sexual adventures. Peer pressure and media glorification are some factors that could lead a teenager to experiment with unknown but exciting zones.

Discussing Sex

It is important to talk about the responsibilities and consequences that come from being sexually active. Pregnancy, sexually transmitted diseases, and feelings about sex are important issues to be discussed. Talking to your children can help them make the decisions that are best for them without feeling pressured to do something before they are ready.

Helping children understand that these are decisions that require maturity and responsibility will increase the chances that they make good choices.

Adolescents are able to talk about lovemaking and sex in terms of dating and relationships. They may need help dealing with the intensity of their own sexual feelings, confusion regarding their sexual identity and behaviour in a relationship. Concerns regarding masturbation, menstruation, contraception, pregnancy, and sexually transmitted diseases are common.

Some adolescents also struggle with conflicts around family, religious or cultural values. Open communication and accurate information from parents increase the likelihood that teenagers will curb their desire to experiment with sex.

In talking with your adolescent daughter, it is helpful to:

- Encourage your child to talk and ask questions.
- Maintain a calm and non-critical atmosphere for discussions.
- Use words that are understandable and comfortable.
- Try to determine your child's level of knowledge and understanding. Keep your sense of humour and don't be afraid to talk about your own discomfort.
- Relate sex to love, intimacy, caring, and respect for oneself and one's partner.
- Be open in sharing your values and concerns.
- Discuss the importance of responsibility for choices and decisions.
- Help your child consider the pros and cons of choices.

By developing open, honest and ongoing communication about responsibility, sex, and choice, parents can help their youngsters learn about sex in a healthy and positive manner.

Some Useful Tips

- You should talk to your teenager about the changes that their bodies are going to go through before the onset of puberty so that they are not surprised by these changes. Your daughter should understand that these changes are normal and there is nothing to get worried about.
- Every mother must educate her adolescent daughter and prepare her gently for what lies ahead. Initially the periods may be scanty or heavy, may occur at three-week or six-week intervals and may be painful or painless.
- A mother must also guide her adolescent daughter about the use and proper disposal of a sanitary napkin, which must always be wrapped in paper and put in a paper or plastic packet before being thrown.
- Adopt a positive and matter-of-fact attitude towards menstruation, which is a perfectly natural phenomenon and a vitally important part of a woman's physical well-being. It is neither an illness nor a painful and uncomfortable time for everyone. A high-strung personality, an illness or anxiety may lead to very heavy blood loss or to skipping of the period, which is why girls need to have an equable temperament and attitude for their physical welfare.

Puberty is also the time when a mother should be well equipped to handle all kinds of emotional and psychological problems that may arise. A well-informed and intelligent mother is more likely to sail comfortably out of the choppy waters with her daughter in tow.

The Queen of the Kitchen

"Food to a large extent is what holds society together and eating is closely linked to deep spiritual experiences."
Peter Farb and George Armelagos
Consuming Passions: The Anthropology of Eating

Without doubt, knowing the art of cooking is indispensable for a girl. Although one hasn't had any spiritual experiences while eating food, there is no doubt that, for a girl, the best way to a man's heart is through his stomach. Which is why you must teach your daughter to cook at an early age.

You could begin by asking her to help you in making *rotis*. Learning to knead the dough is one of the first things a girl should know. If she has an aptitude and fondness for cooking, it will not be long before she masters this. However, as a doting mother, your intention is not simply to teach your daughter to make *rotis*, but prepare a variety of *rotis* and the best ones at that.

Once again, you resort to tips and simple tricks of the trade. For instance, let your daughter know that if serving the food is some time away, then she can simply half roast the *rotis* and pile them up. The final roast can then be done just before serving them. This ensures the *rotis* are piping hot and more appetising than the ones made and kept for a few minutes or more.

Your daughter can also learn to make *rotis* with different fillings every day. Variety being the spice of life for a man, as and when she is married, her husband will love the variety in food, since other kinds of varieties in life are best not encouraged. For instance, *methi*, *paneer*, mashed potatoes, thick spicy *chutney*, *gobi* and other suitable vegetables could be used as filling. Many variations are possible if you and your daughter use your imagination. All the dough circles can be prepared first. The filling can then be spread over the layered *roti*. Apply ghee and fold the roti. Dry flour should then be applied to each *roti* to ensure they don't stick together.

Likewise, in every aspect of cooking, teach your daughter to use simple tips to make a difference in the dish. Something as simple as a cup of tea could be a beverage the man of the house looks forward to. For a few days, or a week, one could use *elaichi* to flavour the tea. The next week, ginger could be used in the tea. Some days you could use fresh ginger and on other days, dry ginger (*sonth*), as each item imparts a flavour of its own. Ginger is particularly good if one has a cold.

The next time around, you could use bundled lemon grass to add a different zing to the tea. Of course, lemon grass and ginger can be used together to spice the tea. But in this case, reduce the quantity of ginger used, so that the tea doesn't taste too sharp and spicy. Also, bear in mind that ginger makes the tea watery, so add more tea leaves or brew for a couple of minutes longer for *kadak chai*.

Hands-on Experience

In the same manner, teach your daughter to cook all kinds of dishes, while also telling her about the variations possible in each dish. Within six months to a year, your daughter should be giving your culinary skills a run for their money. In order to speed up her learning, you could reserve one day in the week, perhaps a Sunday, when she takes charge of the kitchen. On that day, breakfast, lunch and dinner will be your daughter's prerogative. While ensuring you a day off from cooking (rare for most housewives, unless they are ill!), it also gives your daughter hands-on experience.

Following the Indian tradition, also teach her about the importance of seasonal foods and the benefits of having specific foods in different seasons. This not only ensures proper nutrition, but also promotes general health.

Again, with the family's health in mind, teach her the importance of cleanliness and hygiene in the kitchen. While learning to rustle up a quick meal is always an asset, this should not be at the altar of hygienic cooking.

Next, teach her the importance of fuel-saving techniques. Whatever can be cooked in the cooker should be cooked that way, since it saves time and fuel. Copper-bottomed utensils are also better conductors of heat, although they may be somewhat heavier on your wallet. When heating anything over the gas stove, ensure the flame does not leap up the sides of the utensils. If it does, reduce the flame. Much of the flame leaping up the sides is wasted, not to mention the risk of your *sari* or *dupatta* coming in contact with the fire.

Finally, tell her all you know about safety tips while using the gas stove. And before turning in for the night, she must ensure she has turned off the gas regulator too.

The Sous-chef

Having done all this and turned your daughter into the sous-chef, you might now feel like patting yourself on the back. If so, perish the thought! Surely you want your daughter to know more about cooking than you do, don't you?

For starters, on her next birthday you could gift her a lovely set of cookery books. There are many good books on cuisine in the market and you could take your pick from Indian, Chinese, Continental and any other type you and your daughter fancy. She could try out these recipes regularly, particularly on the days when she is The Queen of the Kitchen. A really good cookery book could impart an edge to her cooking that everyday cooking cannot.

Once she is through with the set of cookery books (and this should take her months, if not a year), you could enroll her in a good cooking class, if she wishes to tuck her fingers into specialised skills like preparing dessert, pastries, cakes, chocolates, ice-creams and the like. The courses done with, her cooking could now be the talk of the street, if not the town!

It's now time for you to relinquish the mantle of "The Queen of the Kitchen" to your daughter and take the role of sous-chef. And believe me, when it comes to culinary matters, there can be no greater pleasure than this for every doting mother...

Although eating out has become a part of modern life, there is still a place for good home cooked meals. If your daughter is able to master a few international dishes, she will earn great cudos later in life. In case she is planning to go abroad, knowing how to cook will be invaluable, as there is no household help and one soon tires of the synthetic flavour of pre-cooked and takeaway meals.

Career Options and Economic Compulsions

𝒶 silent revolution has taken place in India during the five decades since independence, one in which women have become educated and are now utilising that by constituting 30 per cent of the workforce. India's first Prime Minister Jawaharlal Nehru would indeed have been elated that his prophecy has been fulfilled as he had written: "…the women's revolution has been neither visibly aggressive and dramatic, but rather after the old fashion in India of combining change with continuity".

In the last 20 years or so, many women have taken up careers in medicine, engineering, computers and management. With every passing day it is becoming more evident that education and training are really the only dowry that a daughter needs. Increasingly, parents are showing their willingness to spend on education and qualifying their daughters in specialised fields. Everyone should invest in a girl-child's education, as it is the only insurance during adverse times for her. Even if she has to return to her father's house after a broken marriage, she need not be an economic burden. She can earn, socialise and, indeed, take care of her parents in their old age.

Eminent sociologist M.N. Srinivas sees the "new woman" as the logical offshoot of the burgeoning middle class and the nuclear family. The XIth and XIIth CBSE Board Examinations show that girls are getting better results than boys, even in subjects like Maths, Commerce and Science. Girls are more career-oriented and are working harder towards achieving their ambition.

Economic Compulsions

Although current inflation rates are unusually low, the decades of the '70s and '80s often witnessed double-digit inflation. The socialist system, unproductive labour and lack of job opportunities presented a grim economic scenario. Those who could, escaped overseas for lucrative careers, but those without these options found the cost of living virtually unmanageable. This was particularly true in the metropolitan cities, where inflation, taxation and the rising cost of essential commodities virtually made double incomes a necessity for the salaried class to meet their monthly commitments.

Reflecting the changing needs of this society in transition are the ubiquitous matrimonial advertisements which reveal that many of today's young men are actually looking for a professionally qualified working girl as a life partner, rather than one who is house-bound.

Today, there is no holding back the Indian woman, for whom all options are open and many of whom view the desire to become doctors, nurses, teachers and lecturers as passé. The increasing numbers of women in the armed forces, the police, the aviation industry and the financial markets are indicative of the fact that they are unlikely to leave any career untouched. As diplomats, civil servants and management trainees, women have entered all professions and are doing well. For example, it seems that Indian women have broken the glass ceiling. When Prime Minister Manmohan Singh went to New York in 2009, both the Indian Foreign Secretary and the Indian Ambassador to the United States were women.

Women in the Workforce

The most striking aspect of the growth of women in the workforce is the easy acceptance extended to them by their male colleagues. Of course, there are issues about discrimination and exploitation at the workplace, but these exist in double measure in the affluent Western countries. I remember reading with absolute outrage that an English lady was sent a male stripper by her male colleagues in the office on her birthday!

Despite being part of a highly traditional, male-dominated conservative society, Indian men have always placed their mother on a pedestal and her domination in household affairs has been part of our culture.

Thus, women in India who were given equal rights at the time of Independence in 1947 were more easily accepted, even in high positions, by male counterparts, unlike women in the West. India has had a woman Prime Minister, and women as Supreme court judges, governors as well as parliamentarians and ministers. Today the President of India is a woman. Compare these statistics with advanced countries like the United States, Japan and Russia in which women have still not been elected to the top political posts till the first decade of the 21st century.

In the corporate world too, women executives in India are actually better off than they would be in American boardrooms. Here they are not yet perceived as a threat. This is because the Indian woman is not aggressively career-oriented. Aggressive feminism in the West has pitted men and women against each other, which is not the case in our country.

Despite the success of women in the workforce, they have not lost their grace and charm. Many take time off to stay home and take care of the children when they are in their formative years, rejoining their careers around forty.

Others manage the balancing act between maternal concerns and career by starting lucrative ventures at home or by taking up flexible careers that do not bind them to a 9 to 5 regimen. Freelance

writing, editing, film-making, tuitions, home catering and tailoring are some of the job avenues being taken up successfully by women operating from their homes. It is important to achieve a balance between career aspirations and the family. Achieving balance has been the key to Indian philosophy. Whether it is *yoga* or *ayurveda*, there is an inherent belief that lack of balance or harmony between different elements leads to disease.

Thus, if one is fired by the desire to earn and achieve, there is no point staying at home and feeling frustrated. At the same time, the family and children are very important and life without them would be empty and meaningless. Often people get so involved with the present that they do not spare a thought for the future. By the time they take stock of the situation, it is already too late. Even if marriage can take place at any age, the childbearing years are limited.

Living with Your Working Daughter

𝒜 new phenomenon has hit Indian society in the recent past. In the urban areas, the marriage age of girls has been on the rise. In earlier decades, it was believed that the prettiest and most eligible girls got married after school! Those who were less good looking went on to college and got married thereafter, while the least attractive looked for jobs in the hope that they would find someone suitable at the work place! Well, today the formula that completely reversed itself, The less privileged study and get married after school, while the most sought after and eligible girls are those who are professionally qualified. Today, a daughter's education is as important as that of a son and girls are eager to work for some time after getting their degrees. Thus in most urban households there is, or there are, working daughters who stay on with the family while they pursue their careers.

While there are many girls from smaller towns who throng the metropolitan areas in search of jobs and live away from home in working girls' hostels or paying guest accommodations and shared flats, a piquant situation arises when your professionally qualified daughter starts working but continues to live with

you. Unlike in the West, when children leave home and seek their own accommodation, families in India prefer to stay together, as far as possible. While there is great joy and jubilation that one child can now stand on her own feet and has become economically independent, the situation arising from this state must be tackled delicately if family harmony is to be maintained. How is this to be done if both parties are to live harmoniously is something which must be understood by all concerned.

A Few Tips for Parents

Your working daughter would be in the age group of 22-23 or even older as the case may be. She is neither in school, nor in college. She is now an adult, who is an earning professional. Hence, parents must restrain themselves from 'helicoptering' or monitoring their every move and phone call. The phrase 'give them space' is a reality, so allow your daughter the freedom of movement and the flexibility of time. Don't closely monitor her movements as her time is no longer her own once she is at work.

Avoid disturbing her at the work place with your phone calls. If at all it is something urgent, send her a message on the cell and await her response.

Allow her the freedom of having a social life without asking too many questions. Give her a house key so that you are not disturbed if she comes in late.

As far as possible, do not probe her personal finances and avoid asking her for money, unless she is ready to give you something. Avoid using her ATM card.

Tips for The Working Daughter

Your parents have worked and sacrificed to make you into a working professional. If your earnings are high, do not adopt a patronizing or superior attitude towards your parents. Always remain respectful and polite towards them.

Remember it is a privilege to remain at home and go to work. Look around you and see the difficulties of those of your friends and colleagues who are living in hired and shared accommodation., or in working girls' hostels. Think of the saving and convenience that you enjoy at home. Thus, if you are earning well and have no educational loans to repay, or even if you do, you may consider setting aside a small amount and giving it to your parents/ mother. In case they do not want anything, you can look around and bring in things for the house, either in terms of foodstuffs or something for the house, such as decorative items, linen, etc.

An extra amount of cash is never unwelcome at any level of society! As the saying goes, "One can never be too rich or too thin!" So, in case your parents refuse a fixed amount every month, you can always compensate by taking them out on birthdays, movies and giving good gifts on Diwali or Christmas and anniversaries.

If you are the eldest and have younger siblings, remember that it means a lot to them to have a working elder sister. Take them out or buy them gifts when required.

Just because you are working and earning, do not acquire unnecessary airs. Remember that the house is a home, not a hotel. Meals have to be prepared and kept for family members. Hence keep the family informed about your timings and whether or not you will be in for dinner.

If you are out, give a rough estimate about the time of return, or sms your mother once you are home.

Adopt the right attitude towards parental concern. As long as you are under their roof, they are responsible for you, so in view of the safety issues in our city, keep them informed of your movements and give a rough estimation of what time you will be home.

The time one spends working and before marriage can be a golden period in the lives of both parents and their daughters. Like in everything else, just a few ground rules and tolerance must be exercised, so that there are no unnecessary glitches. So take full advantage of these years which will take the bonding with your parents to a new level of love and understanding.

A Suitable Spouse

A popular television serial brings to the fore the millions of child brides in the country, particularly in Rajasthan. The girl child in India, especially among the rural poor, is still pushed into early marriage and are even married off to men old enough to be their grand father! However, the urban educated girl is gradually getting a better deal, although the question of dowry harassment being abandoned and ill-treated by NRI husbands is still a big problem.

With higher education and professional qualifications, finding a suitable spouse has become even more difficult. The professional marriage 'go-betweens' has given way to newspaper advertisements and endless sites on the internet. Increasingly, young couples are 'meeting' and 'finding' each other on the net. Initially, the parents prefer to select someone from the same caste and community, but the more enlightened are looking at common backgrounds and common professions in selecting a suitable husband. Due to the increased professional involvement of girls, some parents ensure that their to-be son-in-law earns more than their daughter, so that there is no ego clash in the marriage subsequently.

How does one find Mr. Right? Times have changed and the days of seeing each other for the first time at the wedding '*mandap*' is no longer applicable to our educated daughters. Whether one meets at the work place or at a party, on the internet or through newspaper ads, the couple should meet each other's families and also go out together before making any decision, based on superficialities such as looks and financial status. There is more to life than appearance and money, although these may have their own place in our scheme of things. Since today couples spend a lot of time together, one should look for compatability and common interests. Love, romance and children alone are often not enough as can be seen in the rising divorce figures. The couple should have realistic expectations from each other. Moreover, there should be acceptance of each other as you are. Nobody really changes too much after marriage, so look for those qualities in your to-be-spouse which you want. If they are not there, move on and look for someone else.

Also take a good look at your husband's family as interaction with them is a must and should be pleasant. If the family background is too different, think again before going ahead. Remember that more than ever before, the old adage, "marry in haste and repent at leisure" holds true in the fast-paced modern world. A broken marriage is a sad event that scars and affects all concerned, so do choose carefully.

At one point the NRI spouse was much sought after, but after the horror stories of foreign wives, ill-treatment, being dumped after marriage and the endless drudgery of life overseas, the NRI dream has been broken.

Many families are still into matching horoscopes. In such cases, allow the horoscopes to be matched before going ahead.

Marriage and Motherhood

$\mathcal{I}$f a family is the most important and basic unit of society, the husband-wife team forms the mainstay of this unit. A happy union between a man and woman is the starting point for a happy family. While at one time marriage was treated as a lifelong partnership between a man, a woman and their families, today too many splinters are wrecking this relationship. Gone are the days when marriage was almost a master-slave relationship and a woman's identity was synonymous with that of her husband.

With increasing education and thanks to the hangover from the women's liberation movement, at the turn of the 21st century the

man-woman equation stands challenged on all sides, worldwide. With increasing economic freedom of women, the decrease in social prejudices, a reluctance to wholly accept the responsibilities of childrearing and a career-oriented mindset, the marital relationship has undergone a sea change. The woman now expects to be treated as an equal partner. The traditional role in which the man was the breadwinner and the woman was the homemaker does not always hold true.

Some of these changes have also affected the man-woman relationship in India. Predictably, more couples now break up as the relationship between a man and a woman is a delicate one requiring great love, adjustment and constant communication.

Marriage can only be a lifelong union if each partner is accommodative and understanding about the needs of the other. Even in an arranged marriage, where the parents select a partner who is from the same caste, community and economic background, there has to be a lot of understanding and adjustment.

Unfortunately, dowry has been playing a very detrimental role in the selection of a life partner. The ever-increasing demands of some parents whose sons are doctors, government officers, engineers and the like have resulted in many girls seeking the career option, so that their parents are not forced to pawn everything to get them married.

Where love marriages are concerned also, although the couple may have met in college or at the workplace, there is no guarantee of success. Many marriages fail due to high expectations, unrealistic demands, lack of tact and understanding, intolerance and selfishness. Some relationships falter due to parental interference. Hence, be it an arranged or a love marriage, success still depends on each partner's attitude. If you are to make the best of it, you must give it all you have. True love, affection, care and commitment are never a waste – they will always come back to you manifold.

The fundamental difference between a Western marriage and an Indian one is that in the former, the wedding is the culmination of love and thereafter the road ahead is often rocky. In the case of an Indian marriage, love happens gradually and, often, after one is married. Thus, marriage is not the culmination, but the beginning of a supportive relationship.

In analysing why some of the briefest marriages are those that follow a long period of cohabitation, Germaine Greer (one of the chief architects of the women's liberation movement) says, "The dynamics of mutual accommodation that propelled a couple's informal cohabitation is unnecessary once marriage has confined them. As both are bound, the power will come to be concentrated in the person more prepared to take advantage of the situation, and that is the male partner. Having been so lucky as to acquire a wife, he begins to take the liberties that husbands have traditionally taken, comes and goes as he pleases, spends more time outside the connubial home, spends more money on himself, leaves off the share of the housework that he may have earlier done.

"She sees her job as making him happy; he feels that in marrying her he has done all that is necessary to make her happy. The less she expects it, the more generous he feels for having done it. To her anxious question, 'Do you love me?' he has an easy answer: 'Of course! Married you, didn't I?'"

For a partnership to be truly happy and successful, there should be an effort to understand and please each other. While traditionally women were brought up to believe that their salvation lay in marriage, boys should also be brought up to respect women and realise that a happy union forms the basis of a balanced and secure future.

Pleasing One's Spouse

- A lot of men perceive women to be nagging, suspicious, moody, unreasonable and unduly materialistic. Behave in a manner that changes this stereotype. Dignity, self-respect and self-control will earn you lifelong respect.

- Never fight over money and avoid extravagance if your husband has a salaried income. Try to manage within the budget and put off purchasing what is beyond one's reach. Remember that material goods are not worth fighting over.

- Try to understand the male psyche and read marriage manuals to gain a better understanding.

- While women are good communicators, there is a time and place for everything. There is no sense in greeting your husband with a mouthful of endless chatter as soon as he returns home from the office. The problems and travails of the day can be discussed later over a cup of tea, when the man is in a more receptive frame of mind.

- Be obliging and gracious if your husband wants you to cook a special dish, accompany him to a social function or entertain guests or his family. Do not get carried away by feminist rhetoric and look for absolute equality at every juncture. By acquiescing gracefully at times one builds up a better bond than through bickering and refusals.

- For a man, the physical side of the relationship is the most important, as it is part of his psyche. While women dream of romance, men are more excited by the prospect of sex. A man is also most vulnerable on this score and easily hurt.

- Good looks, good grooming, a good voice and charming manners are a great asset and should be cultivated.

- Be a pleasant companion – the lady of the house largely creates the atmosphere at home. Many wives complain that their husbands do not converse with them or spend time at home. How can they if every conversation is an unpleasant tirade of complaints? Be well-read and aware of current happenings so that conversation with your spouse can go beyond domestic trivialities.

- Do not seek praise and compliments everyday. While it is true that everyone seeks appreciation and would like to be praised, undue vanity on this front results in discord. One wife wanted to be praised for the dishes she prepared and thought that her husband should bring her flowers frequently. When this did not happen, she became disgruntled and dissatisfied. It was not enough for her that her husband relished whatever she had prepared.

- Avoid being over-possessive, unduly suspicious and overly resentful. Over-possessive wives become upset with their husbands if they lavish attention on the children, particularly the daughter. As an adult, have cool confidence and do not seek constant reassurance from your husband.

- Avoid being the I-told-you-so type and be sympathetic even after your husband has fallen ill or suffered because he did not listen to your advice.

- While endeavouring to keep a beautiful house, do not turn cleanliness into a fetish that makes family members uncomfortable. A house is beautiful only if those who are in it live amidst congenial surroundings. If people are always too worried about the carpet, the knick-knacks and the bed cover, when will they relax?

In guiding your daughter about marriage, experts mention a few helpful points.

1. Avoid criticising his family.
2. Avoid telling him that he doesn't love you.
3. Do not tell him that he is not as bright as you are.
4. Do not tell him that you can earn more than him.
5. Avoid criticising his dress sense, appearance and figure.
6. Avoid making comparisons with other men.

7. Don't go on telling him that other men find you more attractive than he does.
8. Show you care by making birthdays and anniversaries special days.
9. The way to his heart may be through his stomach, so do not hesitate to pamper him by cooking his favourite dish.
10. Be unselfish and unconditional in your love. Put the other person before your own needs and pave the way for a happier relationship.
11. Time plays a great role in bringing a couple closer. Going through the ups and downs of life strengthen marital bonds and couples become attuned to each other.
12. Avoid discussing the shortcomings of your spouse with friends or family, as this does not motivate the person to change for the better. Rather, he may feel offended at being discussed behind his back. The best way to bring about change is by explaining his shortcomings patiently and calmly. Rough words will only make him more adamant and averse to improvement.
13. Do not lose your temper simultaneously. If he is already angry, it is better to remain calm until tempers are under control and then resolve the issue.
14. Avoid disagreements, arguments and fights in front of others. One should always strive to maintain dignity and self-restraint.

Dealing with the In-laws

In India, it is said that one does not marry a man but his entire family! This is why utmost care is exercised in selecting a daughter-in-law, as it is felt that her entry into the family can trigger friction.

Due to the existence of the joint family in earlier times, a girl was brought up very strictly so that she did not bring dishonour to her parents by creating discord within the family she married into. Girls were exhorted to be patient, tolerant and silent even under severe provocation. In the rural areas this still holds true, but the educated girl is now taught not to tolerate any kind of real or perceived injustice.

However, rigid behaviour from either side is detrimental. It is a disgrace if a girl is tortured and thrown out of her in-laws' home either because of insufficient dowry or because she has not produced sons. At the same time, your daughter should not be the cause of family discord.

While the daughter-in-law should definitely adjust to her husband's relations, they too should be loving and patient with her as she adapts to her new family. By making her feel welcome they will get a far better response than by carping criticism at every stage.

A mother-in-law should accept the fact that while a son may remain dutiful towards her, he may transfer a lot of loving attention to his new bride, which is as it should be. There is actually no clash in the roles of a mother and wife, if both shed their egos and jealousies, as no one can replace the mother or the wife, since their roles are so different.

It is important for the daughter-in-law to understand that everyone in her new home may be different from her parents and siblings and she should accept this with good grace. Accept people as they are and through good behaviour they can be won over.

Avoid using harsh words and speaking badly about relatives. It is better to keep quiet than speak badly about others.

Accept the foibles and idiosyncrasies of others, especially elders, with good grace and humour. Do not be over-sensitive and overreact to every comment and situation.

Try not to be over-possessive about your husband – remember that he still has some obligations towards his mother and the rest of his family.

A college educated or working girl may not think it is important to maintain good relations with her in-laws, but this is not a healthy attitude. By adjusting with one's in-laws and tactfully handling any criticism or unpleasant situation, one will have a better relationship with one's husband.

Useful Tips

1. Do not enter marriage with the idea of opposing the in-laws. Take the situation as it comes and try to steer clear of conflict.
2. Tolerance and accommodation help in the long run. One should try to create harmony in the household rather than discord.
3. The daughter-in-law should adopt a respectful and helpful attitude towards her mother-in-law. If she does not like something, it is best to voice her feelings diplomatically.
4. Iron out differences with your mother-in-law on a one-to-one basis, rather than by involving others. It is particularly difficult for a man to choose between his wife and his mother, but at some point of time it may become essential for him to intervene, depending on the situation. So keep this to the minimum.
5. The daughter-in-law must try to adjust to her new environment without expecting everything to be as it was at her parental home. She should try to understand and imbibe the customs and traditions of her new family.
6. If the Indian family is to remain united, it is essential that mothers-in-law and daughters-in-law strive to maintain family harmony through self-restraint, love, tolerance and patience – attributes that were always valued in our culture, but are today being devalued due to increasingly individualistic and selfish trends.

Tips for Parents

1. The relationship with one's son-in-law must always have an element of formality and the in-laws must be cordial and pleasant.

2. As parents of the girl, avoid interfering in her household. Never attempt to flood your daughter and son-in-law with gifts, which will make your son-in-law feel he is being undermined. The Hindi film *Kora Kagaz* is an ideal example of interference by the girl's parents, which ultimately brought about discord in the marital life of the young couple.

3. Do not intervene and take sides in petty quarrels.

4. Do not try to monopolise the grandchildren and make them a bone of contention with the paternal grandparents.

5. Do not repeatedly visit your daughter and stay in her house for long periods, as this will cause conflict with her in-laws. Avoid the pitfalls of interference in her life.

6. Do not concern yourself with the day-to-day activities in your daughter's house. What she is cooking, whether her maid came or not, where is she going, should no longer concern you. Cultivate detachment and thank the almighty that you have willingly settled her to find happiness in her own house.

7. Today, the mother of the girl, rather than the mother of the boy is the new villain in marital discord. Hence avoid the trap of being over zealous and over protective.

In a situation where one is living in a modern joint family, elders should not be too rigid and must allow the younger generation to socialise and move about freely. Let them enjoy their independence and give them privacy.

The Place of Motherhood

There are few cultures in the world where the role of mothers and motherhood is eulogised as it is in Indian culture. Speaking on this issue, Mrs Maya Chakraborty, an eminent educationist and ex-Principal of the Naval Public School in Delhi (who has wide exposure to living in both Europe and America), says, "In the West, a woman is regarded more as an object and a symbol. Once she becomes a mother she loses her appeal as a sex symbol and is no longer so attractive to the opposite sex. In India, a woman gains status once she becomes a mother."

For one thing, relationships in the West are both fragile and transient, as couples drift in and out of them. Divorce is easy and variety is the spice of life. When a friend accompanied her husband for a course to Swansea University in Wales, she was often asked how long she had been married. When she replied, "Fourteen years", people looked at her in astonishment and asked, "To the same man?" When she replied in the affirmative, their response, "How boring!"

In India, marriage is considered to be a commitment for lifetime. Only extreme provocations may lead to a divorce and when a couple break up there is considerable social stigma attached to it.

Motherhood and children therefore occupy a pivotal role in the lives of people in India. This does not mean that there is no divorce, unhappiness and incompatibility, but there are many social and family pressures on the couple to remain together. The stigma of divorce is something people do not want to subject their children to.

In the West, high expense, impermanence of relationships and the personal vanity of women have relegated motherhood to the back burner, resulting in negative population rates and an ageing society where there are fewer children.

In India, in the days gone by, life was harsh, with diseases and epidemics rampant, hence people believed there was safety in numbers and had many children. Today, this thinking is changing and the entry of women in the workforce has resulted in single-child families. The nuclear family and DINKs are here to stay. Satisfied with their high incomes and professional commitments, they are the extensions of Western thinking in Indian society.

Recognising the role of women thousands of years ago, Manu restricted women's freedom in certain spheres in order to preserve the family structure. Thus he said, "The mother exceedth a thousand fathers in the right to reverence."

Marriage and motherhood were accorded highest priority and it was the father's foremost duty to marry off his daughter, as there was a belief that a woman could not enter heaven without getting married, no matter how virtuous she might be. Marriage was the very basis of life and motherhood entitled a woman to the greatest happiness both in this life and the next. Children sanctified the union between husband and wife, which is why the husband of a childless woman or one who bore him no sons was allowed to remarry.

No less a person than India's first woman Prime Minister Indira Gandhi said, "To a woman, motherhood is the highest fulfilment. To bring a new being into this world, to see its tiny perfection and to dream of its future greatness is the most moving of all experiences."

Modern medicine has now proved what our ancients knew by instinct, that the female body was created to bear children and health problems abound when these functions are not utilised. The instinct to nurture has been very strong in our culture and parents are motivated by a great desire to see their children prosper.

Working Wives

On account of women's education, their economic emancipation and the ever-increasing cost of living, many husbands have working wives. In such a situation, a man will have to decide before marriage whether he wants a working or non-working wife. The girl also has to ascertain how keen she is about her own career. The couple should jointly decide this so that there is no misunderstanding later on.

While the extra pay packet is always welcome, certain compromises and adjustments must be made in those households where the lady of the house has a full-time career. She cannot completely disown her domestic responsibilities; at the same time she cannot neglect her office work. Many opt for teaching jobs, either in schools or at the college level, as these allow domestic duties to be fitted in as well.

In office jobs, particularly those that are transferable, a lot of compromises have to be made both by the couple and their children. Fortunately, reliable domestic help is still available in India, so one should invest in good full-time servants. Alternately, one would have to depend on one's own mother or mother-in-law to extend a helping hand.

As part-time jobs are not so easily available in our country, particularly since the employment market is already clogged, some ladies opt to work from the home so that they can supervise their homes while exercising their creativity at the same time. To this end, many ladies run crèches, cooking or tuition classes, catering, beauty parlours or boutiques from home.

Ultimately, every person has to decide for herself about how best to combine domestic roles with a career. The increasing rate of divorces, as also delinquent children, is often traced back to a neglectful wife or mother.

One should therefore ensure that money, status and ambition do not come in the way of domestic happiness and family life. A job is not always a substitute for a fulfilling family life. Besides, when both partners are working, they must also work extra hard to keep their marriage from being buffeted by adverse forces.

In an article entitled, "Yuppily Married", Sreelatha Menon writes that Delhi's Double Mobile Couples or yuppie couples are very much on the fast track with their seven-figure salaries and though there is lack of time for each other, they are nevertheless very much in love with one another.

Fashion designer Rina Dhaka offers another take: "Too much time together can create annoyance and dependence. I prefer companionship and compatibility to the illusion of romance in marriage."

Amongst many urban women today, there is also a desire to shun boring domestic chores and a servant is employed to do the needful.

In an article titled, "No sex please... We're married", Prabha Chandran writes that the work-hard-play-hard formula chosen by many urban couples in search of professional and social success is affecting the physical relationship in marriage. Psychiatrists and therapists report that there is a rising crisis in the incidence of platonic marriages in Indian metros. Youthful, urbane and successful, Indian yuppies have paid a huge emotional price for their seemingly enviable international and materialistically successful lifestyles. They may have two thriving careers but opt for one child, a reflection of the sort of readjustment in personal priorities in which the family is no longer the centre of one's life.

While professional success and social standing is a big pay-off, this is often a curiously hollow achievement in terms of personal happiness. Says Dr Alok Chopra from Delhi's Ashlok Nursing Home's stress clinic, "When we start probing the causes of depression, anxiety and many physical ailments from ulcers to backaches, we invariably find we are dealing with an asexual marriage."

While some partners seek solace in spirituality and abstinence, others seek thrills in either clinching deals or in extramarital flings, which are more "exciting" than making love to one's spouse. Others say the change in the marital equation has led to psychologically castrated men.

Therefore, while opting for a career after marriage, one has to weigh all the pros and cons before taking a final decision.

The Working Mother

There is absolutely no substitute for the love and care a mother bestows on her child. Breastfeeding strengthens this bond between mother and child and bottles are no substitute for mother's milk. Since careers are often top priority for a working woman, she either delays having children or marries late – which affects both childbearing and childrearing.

In the West, for example, the increasing rates of divorce, working women and low importance given to domestic life have resulted in a falling birth rate. In Japan too, the growth rate is negative. Since by tradition Japan was a male chauvinist society, today's educated young Japanese woman prefers her independence and sticks with her career rather than marriage and children! To counter this, many countries are giving working mothers as much as a year of maternal leave so that they can care for the child in the crucial early months. The argument of quality time versus quantity time is simply absurd. As far as babies are concerned, they require many hours of devoted care. It is only an older child who can be fobbed off with 'quality time'.

In India, there are neither enough crèches nor is a woman given more than three months' maternal leave. Servants are often used as substitutes and sometimes a mother or mother-in-law has to pitch in and help. It is said that former US President John Kennedy's excessive womanising and callous attitude towards women could be traced back to his hard, cold and frequently absent mother Rose Kennedy. And it is felt that Prince Charles of England and two of his siblings have had broken marriages because the Queen was an absentee mother who did not believe in hugging and kissing her children. Perhaps this is why the late Princess Diana called her husband Charles "an emotionally-constipated Windsor".

Furthermore, in the West there have been many mishaps due to baby bashing. Nannies have not always been a good substitute for the mother.

In India too, it is not advisable to leave a baby exclusively in the charge of a maidservant. At the same time, it may not always be possible for a relative to come and help out over a long period. The problem is especially acute in a nuclear family.

Some Tips

- Working women must carefully consider the pros and cons before opting for a child. Renowned paediatrician Dr Subhas C. Arya states unequivocally in his book: "Your going out to work is usually not in the child's best interest. But there are exceptions. It may be financially necessary for you to work in order to supplement your husband's income. Or you may be a doctor or a highly qualified person who feels the need to work."

- Prime Minister Benazir Bhutto of Pakistan went through two pregnancies even when she was the head of government! Women can do it, but the point is not everyone can, since they are not equipped stand the strain of a baby and a professional commitment simultaneously, as a new mother also requires rest to recuperate from childbirth. Sometimes working women opt to have their babies when they are older and this decision brings in its wake new dangers to maternal health, such as difficulty in conceiving and delivering the child, pregnancy-related high blood pressure and high blood sugar.

- In a nuclear family a reliable nanny is a must. Also, if there is a girl-child it is best not to expose her to male domestic help as instances of child abuse occur.

- The nanny must be kept under close supervision and one should try to drop in for lunch or come in unexpectedly to ensure everything is alright.

- The nanny must possess a good health, as small children are vulnerable to infections. A working mother who had entrusted her son to a maid found to her horror, after a few months, that the maid had contracted tuberculosis. A nightmarish round of doctors and tests followed for all members of the family.

- Make sure you are always in telephonic touch with the house in case of emergencies. Keep a doctor's phone number handy with the maid.

- The working mother comes back to the home tired and it is at this time that the child, craving attention, is at his or her worst. She has to look after the child and see whether or not s/he was properly cared for during the day. She also has to take care of the household chores ranging from laundry to cooking. At this time, if the husband also demands attention, it adds to her woes and fatigue. Therefore, the spouse of a working woman should be helpful in trying to lessen her burden.

Today, social and financial pressures necessitate a woman to take up a job. A frequently asked question of today is: "Are you working?" Many do not believe that homemaking and motherhood are full-time responsibilities! A housewife or mother, however, should not feel bored, frustrated or inadequate as she is doing something that no one can substitute for.

In an article entitled, "What is a smart woman like you doing at home?" Linda Burton articulates the feelings of working women by writing: "I hadn't intended to stay home. Before the birth of my first child, I had a full-time job as a fundraiser at a public interest law firm. It was harrowing for some time, but fun, and it made good use of my energies. After my child was born, I found myself at the age of 33, walking the floor with my son, getting angry about all the things he was keeping me from doing. I missed my job and my friends; I felt poverty-stricken and I looked awful. So, like many other women, I decided to go back to work. I found a job, writing for a television station and happily set out to enjoy life again. I would give my child 'quality' time in the evenings and found an absolutely sterling person to care for him during the day!"

She concludes after giving an account of her experiences with expensive nannies and day-care personnel. "My search for child care taught me a critical question: No matter how many licences we issue, how many guidelines we establish or how much money we pay, it is impossible to have quality controls over the capacity of one human being to love and care for another.

"I had wanted someone who was loving and tender with a sense of humour and an alert, lively manner – somebody who may encourage my children, take them on interesting outings, answer all their little questions, and rock them to sleep. Slowly, painfully, I came to a stunning realisation: the person I was looking for was right under my nose. I had been desperately trying to hire me! And that is what a smart woman like me is doing at home."

In the West, family relationships have suffered and are fairly matter-of-fact. The children are placed in crèches and schools. By sixteen, they are expected to set up their own establishments and become self-supporting. From this point, parental bonds are loosened.

Years later, the children in turn place aged parents in day-care centres and old age homes, when they are too old and infirm to stay on their own. Even persons of Asian origin adopt the same practices due to the lifestyles and compulsions abroad.

Early bonding with the mother is therefore of great importance in order to build security and attachment. While for many in India a whole-time career is a necessity, one must make certain concessions for the child:

1. Try to take as much leave as possible, after the baby is born. Some companies allow extension of maternity leave against loss of salary.

2. Take a part-time job instead of a full-time one, which will be less exhausting.

3. Choose something close to the house so that too much time is not spent in tiresome commuting.

4. Carefully choose the nanny and crèche before entrusting your child to their care.

5. Be happy in whatever you are doing.

6. Do not overindulge a child in order to substitute for your absence.

7. Spend time with the child after your return.

8. Some children resent their mother's absence due to work. Explain why you do so and do not get bulldozed into feeling guilty if it gives you intellectual and financial sustenance.

9. Make foolproof arrangements before leaving your child. Remember the words of Jacqueline Kennedy Onassis: "If you bungle raising your children, then nothing else you do really matters very much."

Today, women must think twice before they either give up their job or continue with it for the sake of their child, after carefully weighing the pros and cons of either decision.

One can only quote the findings of researchers of North London University, broadcast over BBC in 1997, which states that children with working mothers are twice as likely to fail their school exams as compared to those whose mothers stayed home.

It referred to "middle-class deprivation" among families where both parents chose to work full-time, despite the benefits of dual income. It concluded that day care and nannies were no substitute for mothers. Boys, in particular, were likely to do worse and exhibit behavioural problems if their mothers worked.

Patricia Morgan of the Institute of Economic Affairs said that the evidence should bring about some rethinking on what was best for their child: "The entire debate has been hijacked by a feminist clique, determined to uphold women's rights; what about the rights of the child? You can always go back to work, but the damage done in the early years can never be rectified."

Sally Witcher, Director of the Child Poverty Action Group, said: "We cannot turn the clock back and say that all mothers should leave work now. We should instead be asking why people are having to work such long hours. We should also look at why our day-care provision is poor."

Seeing how the family system's destruction has led to so many social, behavioural and addiction problems in the West, we should think carefully before we shun our domestic commitments for money and career ambitions.

Long-distance Marriages

With more women joining the workforce in high-profile careers, the incidence of long-distance marriages is rising. This is particularly true of those in government service such as the IAS, the Foreign Service, the Indian Police Service and those who are with banks and other commercial organisations.

Though these couples are devoted to each other, they are equally or more devoted to their careers and thus have to conduct long-distance marriages. It is something they were mentally and physically prepared for when they entered the relationship.

At the Lal Bahadur Shastri National Academy of Administration, Mussoorie, many marriages between those in service took place. Even if both belonged to the IAS or Foreign Service, let alone if they belonged to different services, couples had to accept the fact that a double income, success and career aspirations had a price attached to it and this the duo in question had to realise and accept.

It was referred to as the problem of the two *chulhas* in which the gains of having a double income were rapidly dissipated when both had to have separate establishments and then strive to meet as often as possible.

In the case of both being batch mates in the IAS, for example, there would necessarily be a period of separation during the initial years, as there are not always two posts of equal rank at the district level. At the senior level it is easier to secure a posting together, either in the state capital or in Delhi. In the interim, the couple must be content with a long-distance marriage with all the pros and cons thereof.

Celebrity couples such as danseuse and Audit and Accounts bureaucrat Shovana Traxl Narayan and her Austrian diplomat husband Herbert Traxl, Foreign Service officer, Nina Sibal and her husband eminent lawyer and Congress activist Kapil Sibal, policewoman Kiran Bedi and her businessman husband, Laxmi and Hardeep Puri of the Indian Foreign Service and many others have made the choices and compromises necessary in such a situation. More often than not, the lady keeps her job as well as takes care of her children, while her husband takes care of himself as a temporary bachelor.

The Advantages

1. A double income and redoubled status.
2. Each person is fulfilling his or her career aspirations, so there is satisfaction on that score rather than frustrated ambitions.
3. Life is one long honeymoon where the couple look forward to being with each other and none of the boredom of living together on a day-to-day basis creeps in.

The Disadvantages

1. There is a period of double expenditure due to running two establishments and frequent commuting to be with each other.
2. There is often great loneliness due to separation and a feeling of helplessness, as all problems and emergencies have to be tackled singly.
3. The togetherness of being a couple is absent and work is the only substitute for loneliness.
4. The children are deprived of being with both parents, often at crucial periods in their life.
5. Physical separation for prolonged periods may result in physical or other relationships with members of the opposite sex or suspicion on this score may arise in either partner.
6. Who will make the *chapattis*? Who will make the tea? The conflict in the working couple's household often boils down to these questions and sometimes the relationship hits rough patches due to this. The ideal solution would be to have a servant to take care of such chores, but if this is not possible, the couple should work out an amicable solution rather than make it a cause for quarrels.

No set rules can be made regarding the above question. There are many men who make the bed tea or wake their wives with a cup of coffee. Some men are better cooks than their wives! Yet others solve the problem by keeping domestic servants. Suffice it to say that the couple should work out their own strategy without resorting to harsh words, gender bias or a rigid stance.

If the double pay packet is welcomed at the end of the month, then the couple must make the necessary compromises and adjustments so that the double income does not lead to double stress in marital relations!

Latch-key Children

This term originated in the West and referred to those children, particularly single-parent ones, who returned home from school, let themselves into the house, ate, watched television and did their homework while their mothers were at work. A similar situation is creeping into many of our urban centres. While smaller children go to crèches after school, those who are older return home and stay alone till their parents return home after work.

Psychiatrists say that 75 per cent of such children have no emotional or behavioural problems, but the emotional development of 25-30 per cent of such children is affected. Dr Achal Bhagat, psychiatrist at the Apollo Hospital, says: "The child of a working mother can get either too independent or too clinging." Dr Bhagat states that in joint families mixed parenting makes the child more loving, trusting and enables it to have a wider vocabulary.

Now a collegian, the only child of a working couple says of his latch-key days: "I learnt to warm the food, do my homework, take down messages from the phone – I grew up fast, but having no one to confide my thoughts to or talk about school often disturbed me."

Children returning from school are at a highly vulnerable stage, as the combination of study and peer pressure makes them want to share their thoughts and frustrations. Most children resent their mother's absence even when they know and realise that she would feel resentful at home. Says a class VI student, "I suppose her career is important to her. If she is forced to give up her job, she will be unhappy and that would not make us happy either."

Children miss their mothers the most when they are sick or during holidays. Doctor Bhagat says: "Children who feel low or depressed or who cry a lot and who complain of non-existent pains are giving out signals of some kind of emotional insecurity." More often than not, it is a ploy to keep their mother at home, as in their own untutored way children are loath to play second fiddle to mama's career!

The pangs of loneliness, rejection, alienation, and isolation are often exhibited in aggressive behaviour and through poor performances in school. While all working mothers cannot give up their jobs, they must be conscious about their parental responsibilities, spend adequate time with the child on their return and strive not to take out the frustrations of a bad day at work on an innocent child. Children must be given time and attention and one can also keep in touch by making phone calls to the child when s/he returns from school.

Finding a Suitable Crèche

It is only in the last decade or so that rising numbers of women are working outside the home and not stopping even after having children. Due to our family system and the availability of domestic help, crèches were not given serious thought. Some social service organisations ran crèches for those women who worked on construction sites. Today, many working women send their children to informal crèches that have mushroomed all over towns and cities.

These crèches are often run by housewives who have some space, the time to spare and wish to earn extra money without leaving their homes. Mrs Vidya Pandit, who runs a crèche from her flat at Khar, Mumbai, asserts that managing kids is not simple. "It does not only mean making them eat tiffins packed by their mothers or putting them to sleep. It means inculcating values in these kids. It becomes our responsibility, especially when th e mothers place such implicit trust in us."

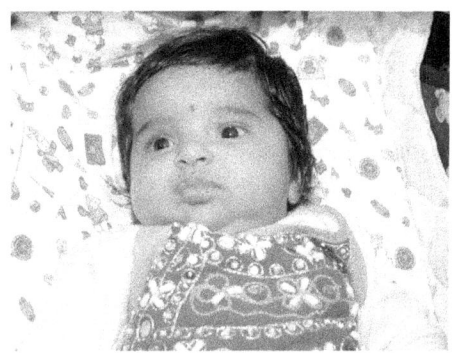

While everyone has acknowledged the need for the crèche, quality control is still not present. One parent alleged that her child became dull as she was administered mild sedatives so that she would not give trouble. After putting her son in a crèche, Divya, a single mother, found that her son had picked up foul language from the other children and the crèche staff. On returning home, he would frequently abuse her with the choicest Hindi swear words. Although all crèches do not take infants, those that do charge high fees and mothers find that frequently the child is left wet or is not cleaned up properly.

The moral of the story – for every crèche that may be observing the prescribed norms of hygiene and sanitation, there are ten that are not up to the mark.

So although crèches are a godsend for the harassed working mother, she should be careful where and to whom she is entrusting her most precious bundle of joy. If one is in a career that is all-important, one should think carefully before deciding to have a baby. But once you have one, it must be looked after with proper care and affection. If it is not possible to make this commitment in time and attention, it is better to forego motherhood than have a maladjusted, neglected child.

Children and their Schooling

The education of children is a major preoccupation for most parents. The difficulty is that with ever-rising numbers, quality education is available only in a limited number of institutions. Parents feel that once their child is put in an English medium school, s/he is made for life. Hence, the lives of three- and four-year-olds are made miserable in the scramble to get into a good school.

In any case, the working mother marches her child off to playschool as early as possible so that the child is able to 'mix' with other children. These playschools and nurseries are basically crèches, but the emphasis is on studies and there is very little play.

The alphabet, numbers, rhymes and more is stuffed into tender minds starting from the age of two or two and a half. Little wonder, then, that many children resist going to school and suffer burnout in class X or earlier. While the playschools claim there are no formal studies, a survey has shown that this is not true. Moreover, many parents want their child to study early, as they believe this would give them a head start in life. But this is not always so.

In the West, and even in Singapore, the schoolbag is getting lighter, while in India it is getting heavier. Every school-going child is taught early in life about the absolute need for success and the bigger the bag, the better the chances of success. In the process, quantity is equated with quality learning.

Earlier, nursery classes of established schools had horrendously difficult entrance exams. Thanks to a campaign in the Press and with better sense having prevailed over some enlightened teachers and parents, this trend has been somewhat checked. While one cannot step back from the rat race altogether, do not put undue pressure on your child in order to get her into a good school.

Some Guidelines

1. Put your child in a school close to your house so that she does not have to commute a long distance.

2. Keep track of newspaper advertisements regarding school admissions, especially at the nursery level, so that you can apply at the right time.

3. Do not chastise your child for failing to secure admission.

4. Schools today want a balanced and emotionally secure child; do not foster tension in the child or she will cry during the admission interview.

5. Do not link your children's success with your own and use their achievements to boast on social occasions.

Inheritance, Dowry and Divorce

The freedom fighters who became rulers of independent India in 1947 were deeply conscious of the fact that a great deal had to be done for the uplift of the people, a significant percentage of whom were women.

Under the leadership of Mahatma Gandhi women had come out of *purdah* and domestic isolation to enter the mainstream of the freedom struggle, picketing, demonstrating and courting arrest. A modern man, with his wide reading and Western education, Jawaharlal Nehru was determined to bring in legislation that would undo much of the wrongs done to women over the millennia.

Thus, the Hindu Code Bill of 1955 was a landmark in emancipating Indian women, at least before the law. While the Constitution of India, promulgated in 1951, guaranteed gender equality, the Bill of 1955 legally armed women with the rights of divorce, inheritance and equal opportunity with men. Polygamy was removed through this legislation and bigamy became a crime. Monogamy became law, although this had never been part of the socio-cultural ethos of the country. Although one cannot say that this aspect of the law has been accepted by all, nevertheless, keeping more than one wife became illegal before the law.

Inheritance

The laws of inheritance also made it possible for women to inherit property from their father, thus overturning the centuries-old tradition of passing it on to the nearest male relative.

Even as pro- and anti-abortion factions battle it out on the streets of American cities, and hundreds of teenaged women die in illegal abortions conducted clandestinely, India made abortions legal as early as 1970-71. Women could have abortions and no questions were asked as it was regarded as her exclusive prerogative to have or not have the child. This liberal law has now become controversial, as abortion and female infanticide have got inexorably linked, resulting in a decrease in the male-female ratio.

An increasing number of women are asserting their independence by seeking redressal for their grievances in court. Way back in 1978, the uproar following the rape of a young *Adivasi* girl in police custody in Mathura led to a landmark decision introducing the concept of "custodial rape". Now, the "burden of proof" lies with the policemen, not with the victim.

A clause widely invoked by legal aid cells was Section 498-A, in which, for the first time, domestic violence against women has been recognised as an offence. This is especially helpful to protect women in dowry cases. Not surprisingly, women's cells have their hands full.

Dowry

One of the most shameful aspects of bringing up a daughter in 21st century India remains the fact that she may become a victim of dowry harassment. Although some amount of dowry or customary gifts was given to the son-in-law at the time of marriage, from the 1970s the problem reached monstrous proportions.

In the social churning that took place as part of the development process, new segments of society rose in the social hierarchy on account of education. The image of a 'spiritual' India was rudely shaken when young brides were doused with kerosene and set aflame by greedy in-laws who wanted all the goodies at the time of their son's marriage. Unfortunately, society is still not free from this scourge and neither has the education of women helped eliminate the problem.

In fact, some amazing aspects became evident when experts looked into the problem. Firstly, the consumer boom exacerbated the problem of dowry-related violence. The degree of greed was greater among the educated affluent, rather than the illiterate poor. Finally, the conviction rate for dowry-related violence in the country was very low.

Since most marriages are arranged, in those cases where the family is unable to fulfil dowry demands, the girl is likely to remain single, despite being educated. The problem is prevalent throughout the sub-continent, from Nepal and Sri Lanka to Pakistan and Bangladesh. In India, there is a visible co-relation between rising prosperity and dowry deaths. An educated girl finds it difficult to find a groom within the community who is as well educated as her.

Statistics tell their own tale of the rising number of dowry harassment fatalities, which keep rising steadily:

Year	1987	1989	2000
Deaths	1,912	4,006	6,222

Many dowry deaths go unrecorded or are categorised as stove burns. Despite the involvement of women's organisations to curb the problem, the conviction rate for this crime is a mere 3 per cent.

Although condemned publicly, dowry continues to be given privately, even by well-placed officials, judges and lawyers. Civil servants and police officials command the highest dowry because of their stature in society.

It is difficult to convict someone under the dowry clause and sometimes many perpetrators go scot-free due to lack of evidence. Many cases are taken to the higher courts by the accused and often the girl's parents invariably lose the will or lack the resources to fight the case till the bitter end.

1000 Plus Household Hints

Tanushree Podder

Often you get bogged down by small problems like moss on the kitchen floor, coffee-stains on the shirt, termite on the new woodwork!

This book endeavours to provide easy solutions to common household problems that crop up from time to time. Designed for the young home makers to help them with the running of the household efficiently, it contains more than a 1000 tips on various aspects of home-management.

Learn how to: * back sparkle on your utensils * eliminate eggy smelling cakes * demoth your woollens the natural way * light up your interiors * get the gloss back on your diamonds and pearls .

So get ready to streamline your housekeeping and your family with clinical efficiency.

price Rs. 150/-, pages 192
size 7.25"x9.5"

Smart Housekeeping for the woman of today

Rupa Chatterjee

A beautiful home is the pride and goal of every woman. In fact, a housewife is very often judged by the way she keeps her house. For her it`s like a temple- a key through which she can ensure the highest level of physical and emotional comfort for her family. And in view of its critical significance in one`s life, it`s imperative that your home is managed well. True it`s an art every homemaker must master.

This comprehensive volume written by a seasoned housewife who is also a professional interior designer, is one such handy help that deals with the subject in a critical and comprehensive manner. Never before so many tips and suggestions, covering every aspect of the subject, have been put together in a single volume.

price Rs. 150/-, pages 292
size 7.25"x9.5"

Beauty solutions
Tanushree podder

This basic book of beauty solutions from top to toe, is meant for every woman with a yearning for a healthy presentable appearance. Some are lucky to be born beautiful, while others can equip themselves with the vast treasure of knowledge provided in this book.

The book presents all the information on beauty in question-answer format.

Many books have been written on the subject but since beauty happens to be the single most obsession with a vast majority of human beings, this book addresses their most common and immediate concerns.

price Rs. 150/- pages 152
size 7.25"x9.5"

Body and Beauty Care
Dr. Neena Khanna

A beautiful face is a letter of recommendation.

Perhaps few things can give you as much confidence as smart and good looks.

This book makes a brilliant endeavour to help beauty conscious to look good and feel confident about themselves.

It gives information on the major categories of cosmetic products with emphasis on intended uses, generalities of formulations and an update on what is new.

*Different skin types, their problems and solutions *The art of make-up through cosmetics *Causes of hair loss and getting rid of superfluous hair through electrolysis *Correction of facial morphology to get a balanced look *Nail and teeth problems and their care *Cosmetic surgery, face-lifts – its scope and limitations *How to tackle weight problems

price Rs. 96/- pages 110
size 7.25"x9.5"

Be Your Own Beautician

Parvesh Handa

This book will tell you exactly how to make and present the best of yourself, how to look radiant from head to feet with the help of natural beauty aids and herbal ingredients. This book describes useful tips for both men and women in detail, to bring out your beauty and explains various questions to the reader.

price Rs.120/-, pages 155, size size 7.25"x9.5"

Herbal Beauty and Body Care

Rashmi Sharma

While the effect of cosmetics is not without harmful consequences, the herbal products are time-tested with a unique blend of several ingredients giving amazing results. The use of these herbal products also encourages women to take up useful exercises daily to ensure proper health and attractive figure. The author has taken every effort to guide the interested reader in creating a new awareness about health and beauty.

price Rs.90/-, pages 144, size 55."x8.5"

Home-made Herbal Cosmetics

Dr. S. Suresh Babu, M.D. (Ayurveda)

Natural herbal products have a definite qualitative edge over chemical-based cosmetics is acknowledged universally today. But then, is every herbal beauty solution as effective as it claims to be? In fact, a lot depends on the extent of knowledge and research gone into its preparation.

Backed by years of research and painstaking effort, this book offers comprehensive solutions — from top to toe.

price Rs.96/-, pages 125, size 55."x8.5"

Parent's Gift to a Child
S. Devraj

The book is aimed at instilling into every child a challenging attitude to dream of even the unlikely with a certainty feeling and to face even the impossible with possibility thinking. This book has a magical power to make every child believe that the easiest to fetch is success and the closest to reach is happiness.

price Rs.50/-, pages 125, size 7"x4.75"

Perfect Marriage not a Mirage
Poonam A. Bamba

Through this book, the author shares real life stories of estranged spouses; What went wrong in their relationship and where? Could the marital relationship in certain situations, have been saved? Perfect Marriage – Not a Mirage also addresses endless doubts which go on in the minds of spouses at the crossroads of their relationship. But at the same time, it also demonstrates that there is no uniform code which can make a marriage work. There cannot be a perfect recipe or a rule book which can guide couples to a successful marriage.

price Rs.150/-, pages 200, size 55."x8.5"

The Secrets of Marital Bliss
Tanushree podder & Ajay Podder

This book gives the readers practical guidelines on how to: *Overcome daily hurdles and live in peace and harmony *Avoid pitfalls that appear at various stages of married life.

Married and unmarried couples of all ages must read this book to ensure peace, stability and harmony in their relationship.

price Rs.80/-, pages 176, size 55."x8.5"

www.ingramcontent.com/pod-product-compliance
Lightning Source LLC
Chambersburg PA
CBHW070334230426
43663CB00011B/2313